HARVARD HISTORICAL MONOGRAPHS

XLIV

Published under the direction of the Department of History
from the income of The Robert Louis Stroock Fund

Foch versus Clemenceau

France and German Dismemberment, 1918-1919

JERE CLEMENS KING

HARVARD UNIVERSITY PRESS
Cambridge, Massachusetts
1960

© 1960, by the President and Fellows of Harvard College

Distributed in Great Britain by Oxford University Press, London

Library of Congress Catalog Card Number 60–11557
Printed in the United States of America

Preface

A soldier who assumes the role of self-appointed peacemaker poses many ticklish problems in civil-military relations, as Marshal Ferdinand Foch demonstrated during the Versailles Peace Conference. The present monograph treats the determined efforts of Marshal Foch to arrange a peace which, according to him, would provide France with security, but which, according to his civilian superior Georges Clemenceau, would have lost France's urgently needed allies.

In a previous work, *Generals and Politicians: Conflict Between France's High Command, Parliament and Government, 1914–1918*,[1] I treated the problems which arose in war time France because of the delay in winning a victory over the Germans. *Generals and Politicians* focused attention upon the battlefield and the arena of French domestic political strife in which the military at first arrogated to themselves the powers of the government; then Parliament invaded the spheres of the government and the command; and finally the government, under Clemenceau, gained ascendancy.

In the period of the Versailles Conference, which is the phase of French civil-military relations treated in the present monograph, Clemenceau's right to negotiate the peace settlement was challenged by the mettlesome hero Foch. Yet the power of negotiating the peace settlement incontestably lay with Clemenceau and his tractable Foreign Minister Stephen Pichon—foreign relations being vested in the government by Article 8 of the Constitutional Law of July 16, 1875. Parliament was in eclipse during the Versailles Conference, so much so that as late as mid-April 1919, five months after the

[1] Jere Clemens King, *Generals and Politicians: Conflict Between France's High Command, Parliament and Government, 1914–1918* (Berkeley, California, 1951).

armistice, some of the deputies felt justified in complaining that "Parliament was informed of nothing," that it was a "deaf and dumb body." [2] These were isolated protests and their very paucity indicated the extent to which Parliament was relegated to the shadows until the ratification debates began on August 26, 1919, two months after the signing of the treaty, when the floodgates of criticism were belatedly opened. French internal conflict in civil-military relations during the Peace Conference was thus primarily between Clemenceau and Foch, both inspired by the most patriotic of motives.

The present monograph takes one into the field of diplomatic maneuvers among France, its allies, and Germany. It sketches the Rhineland separatist movement in 1919 as incidental background to the momentous struggle between Foch and his field commanders on the one hand and President of the Council Clemenceau on the other over their differing conceptions of a realizable peace which could guarantee France's security. But, as compared with the war years, the cast was reduced by the absence of Parliament during this phase of the politico-military drama, except for the postlude.

I wish to express my gratitude to the Center of International Studies, Princeton University, and to the Committee on Research, University of California, Los Angeles, for generously assisting me in undertaking this monograph.

J. C. K.

---

[2] France, Assemblée nationale. *Annales de la Chambre des Députés, débats parlementaires* (Paris, 1919) . . . Séance du 16 avril, 1919, I, 1780–1782.

Contents

Foch Versus Clemenceau

Chapter I

The French Watch on the Rhine

What is the proper course for an illustrious soldier who has just won a war and who sees the "frock coats" of his government arranging a peace settlement which he considers disastrous? Such was the quandary confronting Marshal Ferdinand Foch during the Versailles Peace Conference in the spring of 1919. Should the military hero press his unsolicited advice upon the perverse peacemakers, or obediently hold his tongue and hope for the best? Should he defy the civil authority in such circumstances? Should he resign his command in protest? Or would he be justified in maneuvering behind the scenes to confront the heedless statesmen with an accomplished fact in diplomacy which would all but compel acceptance of his military solution?

Foch, with impeccable patriotism but dubious wisdom, tried in succession all five of these tactics in his determination to emasculate Germany by bounding the nation at the Rhine. The numerous war time conflicts between Foch and his civilian superior, Georges Clemenceau, broke out anew over this complex question. The gradual relinquishment by the President of the Council of France's demand for a detached Rhineland in the face of Anglo-American opposition appeared to Foch as no less than a betrayal of public trust. The marshal became so exercised over Clemenceau's "capitulation" to Washington and London that he tried to "save" the peace by moving into the policy-making role. The usual term for such an act is insubordination, but Foch's patriotic intentions and the frustrations of French public opinion allowed it to be condoned.

It was only natural for Foch to show a keen interest in a detached

Rhineland, since this surgical solution to the German problem had a strong appeal for perhaps most Frenchmen with the exception of the Socialists. But, in parliamentary and governmental circles in Paris, before and during the hostilities of 1914–1918 as well as during the peace discussions, it was understood that the voicing of French desires to annex the Rhineland, or to create buffer states there, or to internationalize it, would precipitate drastic German reaction. During the ratification debates, the most ardent advocate of cutting off Germany at the Rhine, the President of the League of Patriots, Deputy Maurice Barrès, admitted to the Chamber of Deputies on August 29, 1919 (at a safe interval after the signing of the treaty): "It was thirty years ago when I first took my seat in this Assembly, but never have I heard a debate on our Rhineland policy. There was no reason for one. When we were on the Vosges and at Briey, the question was not raised. But today it is different! We can no longer evade the issue now that we are at Wissembourg, Saarbrücken, Thionville." [1]

Barrès' recollection in regard to parliamentary reticence was substantially correct, although he overlooked an isolated occurrence on December 29, 1918, when Socialist Pierre Renaudel blurted out the remark that it was conceivable that "sensible" Germans on the Left bank of the Rhine might wish to avoid reparations levies by "detaching themselves from Germany." This unexpected broaching of the most delicate of proposals—and that by a Socialist and a leading member of the party which was understood to be opposed to annexation—brought immediate correction from Renaudel's fellow leftist, Deputy Mayéras: "I repeat that I am among those who will oppose any attempt at even a disguised annexation of the Left bank of the Rhine." Renaudel hastened to explain, "Whatever solution may be contemplated . . . the only formula applicable to territorial readjustments is one based upon the wishes of the people." [2]

Apart from this Freudian slip, the parliamentarians observed a calculated silence in regard to the Rhineland until the treaty was signed. Nor did Parliament debate *in camera* the detachment of the

[1] Maurice Barrès, *Les grandes problèmes du Rhin* (Paris, 1930), p. 3.
[2] *Annales de la Chambre* . . . Séance du 29 decembre 1918, I, 3348. On parliamentary reticence, see also *Le Temps*, March 30, 1919.

Rhineland, since the secret committees had fallen into abeyance in 1917, and Clemenceau would not agree to their restoration. On December 2, 1918 the Foreign Affairs Commission of the Chamber of Deputies did draw up a resolution in favor of detaching the Rhineland, but it merely submitted this memorandum to the government for its instruction. It did not formally present the proposal to Parliament for action. Similarly, the parliamentary Treaty Commission, with the historian and member of the Institute, Deputy Charles Benoist, serving as *rapporteur,* recommended to the government the drawing of France's military frontier at the Rhine. But, as in the case of the Foreign Affairs Commission, the Treaty Commission made this recommendation confidentially to the government. Only during the ratification debates, lasting from August 26 until October 2, 1919, did Parliament venture to publicize its views on the kind of frontiers which the treaty ought to confer upon France.

No such sapient restraint was exercised by private French citizens. Hardly had the war broken out when there began to appear (with the censor's benediction) a spate of inflammatory books on France's role in the Rhineland in the past and future. The geographer Onésime Reclus published a volume, *Le Rhin français. Annexion de la rive gauche. Sa moralité. Sa necessité. Ses avantages,* in which he threatened the Germans with a "colossal" war indemnity, and in addition, with the establishment of a French protectorate and customs union in the Rhineland patterned on Tunisia and Morocco. This solution would have many advantages for France, among them the removal of predatory Germany to a much safer distance from Paris. The Rhinelanders, thus "freed," would be won over to France by benefactions which had been so successful with the Moroccans. "We do not regard the Cisrhenians as pure Germans in the sense of the Prussians, but as half-French, as half-brothers, whom we wish to bring back into the family." Reclus, in a second work, *L'Allemagne en morceaux: paix draconienne,* was willing to grant the Cisrhenians three choices: annexation to France, a French protectorate, or independence. But, if the Rhinelanders should choose independence, it would be on the condition that they would be "neutralized by Europe." Reclus believed that the Cisrhenians would be intelligent enough to perceive the advantages of being freed from

Prussian "brutality"; of belonging to the generous "land of good wines"; of having the opportunity to work in France and to assist in the colonizing of Africa; of being freed from the future war indemnity which Germany would have to pay. Assimilation with the French language and culture would be easy and gradual: each Rhineland village would "have its school where anyone who wished could learn [French], not from an enemy, but from a friend." [3]

Abbé Stephen Coubé, in *Alsace, Lorraine et France rhénane: exposé des droits historiques de la France sur toute la rive gauche du Rhin,* claimed the Rhineland for France by virtue of ancient historic rights. Coubé contended that Rhenish Bavaria, Rhenish Hesse, and Rhenish Prussia "belonged to us in the Celtic, Gallo-Roman, Merovingian and Carolingian epochs. German on the surface, their population, especially in the countryside, is deeply Gallic in soul and blood. . . . One must not annex what belongs to another, but one can—one should—repossess what is his own property when one has been despoiled by a thief." The Cisrhenian provinces should not be left to Germany, since they would serve again as a springboard of invasion by way of Belgium and Luxembourg. The abbé quoted Napoleon with approval: "The boundary of the Rhine, like the Alps and Pyrénées, is a decree of God." Coubé excoriated the Socialists with their pacifist slogans of "No conquests! No annexations!" by reminding them that the fixed idea of such revolutionary deities of theirs as Danton, Carnot, and Siéyès, as well as a later generation of advanced thinkers such as Thiers, Louis Blanc, Edgar Quinet, Barbès, and Blanqui, "was to reunite all the Left bank of the Rhine with France. They claimed it not as an annexation or conquest but as a restitution or recovery of our property." The shades of the great ancestors turned in their graves with indignation "at the thought of epigoni who repudiated their program." [4]

---

[3] Onésime Reclus, *Le Rhin français. Annexion de la rive gauche. Sa moralité. Sa necessité. Ses avantages* (Paris, 1915), p. 77; *L'Allemagne en morceaux: paix draconienne* (Paris, 1915), pp. 28–29.

[4] Abbé Stephen Coubé, *Alsace, Lorraine et France rhénane: exposé des droits historiques de la France sur toute la rive gauche du Rhin* (Paris, 1915), pp. 4, 5, 25, 179, 180.

C. M. Savarit, in *La frontière du Rhin,* found in the very title of one of Germany's most sacred national anthems, the *Wacht am Rhein,* an oblique acknowledgement that the great river was the proper boundary of the German people. As for the objection that the Rhinelanders speak German and therefore should belong to Germany, Savarit asserted that the Alsatians, Bretons, and Basques were no less French for their use of "foreign" tongues. Beneath the linguistic veneer of Germanism, the Rhinelanders had a millennial heritage based upon "Ligurian, Gaulish, Gallo-Roman, Frankish, and Christian tradition—which is to say French." Savarit conceded that an independent, buffer republic might be constructed in the Rhineland, but he thought it would be militarily weak, without geographical unity or historical foundation. "All these reasons suggest only one rational, humane and peaceful solution to the question of the Rhineland provinces—their reunion with France and Belgium." [5]

That the dominant strain of the Rhinelander was Celtic and Gallo-Roman, with Germanism being only a recessive characteristic of relatively recent origin, was equally the conviction of Abbé Wetterlé in *La jeune generation en Alsace-Lorraine,* [6] and Major Espérandieu in *Le Rhin français.* Espérandieu believed that French annexation of the Rhenish population was only a question of time, and that it would be desired by the inhabitants themselves, once the indoctrination of the German schoolmaster had worn off. [7]

The stereotyped theme that the Rhineland people were Gallo-Roman and Frankish in origin, with their Germanism only a recent overlay applied by the Prussian schoolmaster, soldier, civil servant, and industrialist, was reiterated by Ernest Babelon in his two-volume work, *Le Rhin dans l'histoire.* Like Major Espérandieu, Babelon looked forward to the time when "nature would reassert itself and would mark the Rhenish population with the Lotharingian impress." Babelon emphasized the need of garrisoning the Rhine, and he hoped that it would be done by the armies of a Western bloc com-

---

[5] C. M. Savarit, *La frontière du Rhin* (Paris, 1915), pp. 26, 28.
[6] Abbé Wetterlé, *La jeune génération en Alsace-Lorraine* (Paris, 1915).
[7] Major Espérandieu, *Le Rhin français* (Paris, 1915).

prising Belgium, Holland, Switzerland, Luxembourg, and the Rhineland itself, as well as France. He felt that if, in addition, England and Italy would agree to an alliance with France, peace for Western Europe would be reinsured.[8]

In *La verité territoriale et la rive gauche du Rhin,* F. de Grailly added his voice to the French demands for the Rhine on the familiar grounds that the region was "an integral part of the land of the Gauls; its population is Gallic by nature and will always be so. . . . One cannot undo basically what nature has done. . . . At best one can change only superficial appearances and even that only temporarily." [9]

Economic historian Georges Blondel, the author of *La Rhénanie: son passé: son avenir,* found in the word Rhine itself, as well as in the ancient names of the tributary streams and the divinities of the Rhineland, an etymology heartwarmingly Celtic. Blondel contended that during the Middle Ages, when the Germanization of the Left bank of the Rhine took place, there was no "German patriotism" in the region. The petty princes, vassals of the Holy Roman Emperor in Vienna, readily accepted the role of pensioners of the Bourbon kings of France long before the conquest of the region by the armies of the Revolution. Blondel was convinced that wherever the French and German temperaments met, "the former always attracted the latter and absorbed it, as the spirit of Rome became captive to that of Greece." This augured well for a Gallicized Rhineland in the future.[10]

Albert de Pouvourville was specific about France's past in the Rhineland, but somewhat vague about its future. In *Jusq'au Rhin: les terres meurtries et les terres promises,* he declared that it was "in the region of the Rhine that the French race was born. . . . It is an error—now recognized—to say that the French came from Franconia; it is worse than an error, it is a German falsehood. The Franks did not come from so great a distance. They came from

[8] Ernest Babelon, *Le Rhin dans l'histoire* (Paris, 1916–17), II, 505.

[9] F. de Grailly, *La verité territoriale et la rive gauche du Rhin* (Paris, 1917), pp. 278–279.

[10] Georges Blondel, *La Rhénanie: son passé: son avenir* (Paris, 1921).

Tongres and the region between the Rhine and the Meuse." For France to move back to the Rhine would be only a homecoming. "So, whatever the means to be employed, whatever the ingenious texts or euphemisms which the diplomats will devise, the French Rhine must become the defensive moat of our great Western fortress. . . . We shall do whatever the populations west of the Rhine desire which is deserving of a régime in conformity with their customs and history, but we need the Rhine against Germany." The inhabitants were thus to have free choice, so long as they chose France.[11]

Misgivings about the viability of a neutral, independent Rhineland state were voiced by the historian J. Dontenville in his volume, *Après la guerre: les Allemagnes, la France, la Belgique et la Hollande*. Such a neutralized buffer state "would be a pure diplomatic fiction, guaranteed by a 'scrap of paper' which an unscrupulous neighbor could tear up at the first opportunity. . . . Germany and France would not be slow to quarrel about . . . a new interjacent state." Dontenville advocated France's outright annexation of the Rhineland south of the Moselle, but, with a display of generosity, he proposed the cession of the Northern Rhineland to Belgium as "compensation for damages cruelly suffered for heroism in upholding European public law." If Belgium should decline the offer, France would appropriate the entire Left bank. Germany east of the Rhine would be split between a Southern Confederation comprising Bavaria, Baden, Württemberg, Hesse-Darmstadt, Frankfurt and Lichtenstein, and a Northern Confederation. The Rhinelanders would be well treated by the French and Belgians who would be "firm" but at the same time "sweetly persuasive." The Cisrhenians would experience a far different fate from the Poles, Danes, Alsatians, and Lorrainers still groaning under German rule.[12]

The French Revolution specialist, Alphonse Aulard, sought in *La paix future d'après la révolution française et Kant* a solution to

[11] Albert de Pouvourville, *Jusq'au Rhin: les terres meurtries et les terres promises* (Paris, 1916), pp. xix, 146, 340.

[12] J. Dontenville, *Après la guerre: les Allemagnes, la France, la Belgique et la Hollande* (Paris, 1915), p. 39.

France's dilemma: "Either we annex the Left bank of the Rhine and violate principle, or we do not annex it and France remains in perpetual danger of invasion." Aulard proposed changing the constitution of the German Empire in such a way as to withdraw the Rhinelanders "from all authority of Prussia" while allowing them to remain German. Aulard did not share the optimism of Wetterlé and Espérandieu about the ease with which Germanism could be deracinated from the Rhinelanders. "We shall not compel them to be French, which they do not wish to be." He advocated setting up a Rhineland Republic as a neutralized buffer state. "We shall force them to love peace. . . . We shall remove from them the means of making war." In contrast to Dontenville, Aulard was not worried over the viability of such a buffer state, nor concerned about its ability to pit France against Germany in future quarrels.[13]

Aulard's distinction between Germany and Prussia was rejected by his fellow historian, Edouard Driault, in *Les traditions politiques de la France et les conditions de la paix*. Driault believed that "Germany, after the atrocities committed, [was] equally an accomplice in the Prussian crime. . . . It ought to suffer punishment along with Prussia. . . . France, installed beside Belgium upon the Rhine, should draft a new Peace of Westphalia." By thus recreating a multitude of Germanies, by restoring the old "Germanic liberties" for which French kings had often served as protectors, a chastened Germany should reëmerge as the land of "great artists and illustrious philosophers." [14] In another work, *La République et le Rhin,* Driault attacked Albert Sorel's thesis that France implanted upon the Rhine constituted a threat to the European equilibrium, which menace had been traditionally met by the raising of one coalition after another for the purpose of pushing France back to its proper boundaries. Driault felt that Sorel had not been brought up to date, for he failed to understand that the more recent "establishment of Prussia on the Left bank of the Rhine had compromised the

[13] Alphonse Aulard, *La paix future d'après la révolution française et Kant* (Paris, 1916).

[14] Edouard Driault, *Les traditions politiques de la France et les conditions de la paix* (Paris, 1916), p. 212.

equilibrium of Europe . . . that the Prussians at Coblenz were a cocked pistol aimed at the heart of France . . . and England." Driault did not advocate an abrupt political annexation of the Rhineland. "We shall not annex the populations of the Left bank of the Rhine to France *without consulting them*." However, he did propose a military occupation, regardless of the inhabitants' wishes, "until the complete fulfillment of all the conditions of the peace." The region should also be bound to France by a customs union.[15]

The Belgian writer Charles Stiénon was requested by the League of Patriots to prepare a book on France's role in the Rhineland. In *La rive gauche du Rhin et l'equilibre européen,* Stiénon emphasized the strategic importance of the region. Like Driault, he called attention to the recent ominous shift in the European balance of power to Germany's advantage. "Until the end of the second half of the 19th century, France on the Rhine seemed a threat to Europe. Now it is France separated from the Rhine which is an inadequate bastion of world peace." It was to the interests of Russia and the other Allies to assist in pushing Europe's center of gravity of population from Germany back toward France to restore an equilibrium destroyed in 1870.[16]

One of the most drastic proposals for solving the German problem came from a Royalist, the art historian Louis Dimier, who published a book with the baldly explicit title, *Les troncons du serpent: idée d'une dislocation de l'empire allemand et d'une reconstitution des Allemagnes.* Dimier advocated the atomizing of Germany—the creation of a hundred or so free cities, including Berlin; the retrocession of segments of the German boundaries to Sweden and Poland; and in the Rhineland and its affluents, the Wupper and Ruhr valleys, the constitution of a republic to be entrusted to the trade unions—a workers' state of the Ruhr-Rhineland. Even Dimier seemed somewhat abashed by his startling proposals as he revealed in a footnote at the end of his introduction: "I believe I ought to mention at the close of this introduction that this book, which is the work of a

[15] Edouard Driault, *La République et le Rhin* (Paris, 1916), p. 147.
[16] Charles Stiénon, *La rive gauche du Rhin et l'equilibre européen* (Paris, 1917), p. 47.

private individual who is not connected with any party in office, in no way commits the French government." [17]

In *La France de l'Est,* the geographer Vidal de la Blache showed considerable ingenuity in justifying France's presence in the Rhineland. He argued that a France located on the Left bank of the Rhine would break Germany's monopoly of navigation in the region. The French could take measures which would "assure to foreign flags—British, Norwegian, American and others—Rhine navigation freed from all fetters." France on the Rhine could bridge a continent which otherwise would be sundered by Germany astride both banks of the river. [18]

The historian of the French Revolution, Philippe Sagnac, posed a series of adroit questions in the introduction of his book, *Le Rhin français pendant la révolution et l'empire.* After a discussion of the Rhinelanders' genius for blending such diverse cultures as the German, French, and Dutch into a harmonious and unique *mélange,* Sagnac asked: "Will these old regions return one day to ancient Gaul and to the Gallo-Roman civilization. . . ? How will the French occupy and organize the country? What feelings will they find among the inhabitants? What assistance and what obstacles will they meet. . . ? How will they finally reunite the country with France, and to what degree will there be assimilation? What, in a word, will be the result of the meeting of the German and French spirit on Rhenish soil?" The French reader of 1917 must have been startled to realize that Sagnac was speculating upon the role which France was to play in the Rhineland in the year 1792, on the eve of the victories of General Custine. [19]

In addition to the efforts of individual authors to advance France's Rhineland claims, there were so-called "scientific" committees engaged in expansionist propaganda. The German writer Friedrich Grimm contended that they were more or less under the clandestine supervision of the Quai d'Orsay, a charge difficult to verify but

[17] Louis Dimier, *Les tronçons du serpent: idée d'une dislocation de l'empire allemand et d'une reconstitution des Allemagnes* (Paris, 1915), p. 10 n.

[18] Vidal de la Blache, *La France de l'Est* (Paris, 1917), p. 231.

[19] Philippe Sagnac, *Le Rhin français pendant la révolution et l'empire* (Paris, 1917), pp. 6–7.

thoroughly plausible. Of chief importance was the Committee of the Left Bank of the Rhine, composed of thirty-six French educators, lawyers, retired admirals, and figures of social prominence. The Committee's principal advisers were Abbé Wetterlé and Maurice Barrès, who also served as President of the League of Patriots. The latter organization sponsored the publication of books, articles, and tracts, the holding of conferences, and the circulation of a large number of post cards to propagandize France's claims on the Rhineland. These propaganda committees enlisted the services of well-known scholars. The Historical Committee was directed by Ernest Lavisse of the Sorbonne; the Michelet Committee by the historian Edouard Driault; the Parliamentary Action Committee by Louis Engerand, archivist-paleographer of the Bibliothèque Nationale.[20]

Although wartime censorship in France was strict, the expression of expansionist views by private citizens in no wise committed the French government. In contrast to the fanfare of publicity attending all these private pronouncements, French officialdom handled the Rhineland question with great caution and secrecy. President Raymond Poincaré proposed to Premier Aristide Briand a plan whereby France could obviate predictable British opposition to a detached Rhineland by reaching a prior understanding with Russia over the division of enemy territory. Paris and Petrograd could confront London with an accomplished fact in their territorial designs and thus nullify British opposition. The parliamentarian Gaston Doumergue was sent on a special mission to Petrograd in December 1916 to treat the ticklish question with the Russian foreign minister.[21]

[20] Friedrich Grimm, *Poincaré am Rhein* (Berlin, 1940), p. 15; cf. George B. Noble, *Policies and Opinions at Paris* (New York, 1935), pp. 19–23; see also Leo Böhmer, *Die Rheinische Separatistenbewegung und die französische Presse* (Stuttgart, 1928), p. 12; also Erich Kaden and Max Springer, *Der Politischen Charakter der französischen Kulturpropaganda am Rhein* (Berlin, 1923), pp. 11–13; also George E. R. Gedye, *The Revolver Republic* (London, 1930), p. 65. For an example of the work of the Committee of the Left Bank of the Rhine, see J. L. Bonnet, *Les restitutions, réparations, sanctions et garanties a imposer a l'Allemagne* (Paris, 1917). For an example of the work of the Parliamentary Action Committee, see Louis Engerand, *L'opinion publique dans les provinces rhénanes et en Belgique, 1789–1815* (Paris, 1919).

[21] Gabriel Terrail [Mermeix, pseud.], *Le combat des trois: notes et documents sur la conférence de la paix* (Paris, 1922), pp. 224–225.

While Doumergue was negotiating, Premier Briand acknowledged France's Rhineland desiderata in a confidential letter of January 12, 1917, to Paul Cambon, the French Ambassador in London. Briand conceded that the "recovery" of the Rhineland would be difficult since it would be considered conquest. But the important thing was to seize the "glorious albeit precarious opportunity" of creating a safeguard not only for France but for Europe. "In our opinion," wrote Briand, "Germany should no longer have a foothold beyond the Rhine. The future status of our Rhineland territories, [the region's] neutrality and provisional occupation ought to be taken up in an exchange of views with the Allies, but it is important that France, as the one most directly concerned . . . should have the preponderant voice in considering the solution of this grave question." [22]

Part of Briand's wishes were to be realized within a few weeks. The Russian government responded to the overtures of Gaston Doumergue: in a secret note written by Foreign Minister Nicholas N. Pokrovsky, the Tsarist regime officially recognized France's right to control the iron deposits of Lorraine and the coal district of the Saar Valley. It also agreed to separate from Germany the Left bank of the Rhine for the purpose of constituting there an autonomous and neutral state, to be occupied by French troops until such time as the enemy completely satisfied all the conditions of the peace treaty. As a *quid pro quo* the French government reassured Russian Ambassador Isvolsky on March 11, 1917 that it fully recognized Russia's claims upon Constantinople and the Straits, and its "complete liberty in establishing its western frontiers." [23]

The secrecy of this diplomatic exchange proved short-lived, for the German Chancellor Bethmann-Hollweg soon got wind of the

---

[22] France, Assemblée nationale. *Annales du Sénat, documents parlementaires* (Paris, 1920) . . . Séance du 3 Octobre 1919, p. 586. See also Georges Vial-Mazel, *Erreurs et oublis de Georges Clemenceau: L'affaire du Rhin* (Paris, 1931), pp. 200–201; Terrail, *Le combat des trois,* p. 193; André Tardieu, *The Truth About the Treaty* (Indianapolis, 1921), p. 161; Guy de Traversay, "La première tentative de République rhénane," *La Revue de Paris* (November 15, 1928), p. 409.

[23] Ray Stannard Baker, *Woodrow Wilson and World Settlement* (Garden City, N. Y., 1922), I, 58; cf. Terrail, *Le combat des trois,* pp. 224–225.

Franco-Russian agreements and publicly charged that France and Russia had drawn up a secret treaty, on the eve of the Russian Revolution, in which the Tsar had promised to support French pretensions to the Left bank of the Rhine. French Premier Alexandre Ribot had to take cognizance of this charge, which he did on two occasions. In a speech to Parliament on May 22, 1917, he specifically repudiated the idea of conquest of German territory. But doubts lingered, and on July 31, 1917, Ribot felt obliged to say to Parliament:

The Chambers know how things happened. M. Doumergue, after his conversation with the Tsar, asked and obtained from M. Briand authorization to take note of the promises to support our claim to Alsace Lorraine, torn from us by violence, and to leave us free to seek guaranties against further aggression, not by annexing to France territories on the Left bank of the Rhine, but by making of these territories, if need be, an autonomous state protecting us as well as Belgium against invasion from beyond the Rhine.[24]

Suspicions of France's intentions to alter the status of the Rhineland were heightened by the Russian Bolsheviks who broadcast over the Petrograd radio in December 1917 the verbatim text of the Doumergue-Pokrovsky agreement (as well as the other wartime secret treaties of the Allies). To all the ingenious private French proposals regarding the Rhineland was thus added the revelation of the official intentions of Paris, although in terms still quite vague.

To learn precisely what his government expected to do with the Rhineland, Marshal Foch addressed a letter to President of the Council Georges Clemenceau on October 16, 1918. He inquired whether there was to be an adequate guarantee of reparations; what would be the future of the Rhineland territory; how long French occupation would continue; whether the region was to be annexed or made into a neutral, independent buffer state; whether Clemenceau would have the Quai d'Orsay assign him a liaison official to keep him informed of the government's intentions.[25] Foch was ready to appropriate and stamp with his vast military prestige a set

[24] Quoted in Ebba Dahlin, *French and German Public Opinion on Declared War Aims* (Stanford University, Calif., 1933), p. 98.

[25] Ferdinand Foch, *Mémoires pour servir a l'histoire de la guerre de 1914–1918* (Paris, 1931), II, 278.

of ideas already becoming threadbare by the time of their possible implementation. Foch did not originate any of the various Rhineland schemes, but he gave the proposals a momentum which no one else could supply.

Clemenceau replied with a rebuke for officiousness which none knew better how to administer. On October 23, the President of the Council sent Foch a letter in which he spelled out his role for him, reminding him that he was only the military adviser to the government, and as such would be consulted only on purely technical matters, with the government being free to accept or reject such counsel as it saw fit. Diplomatic and economic aspects of the Rhineland question were beyond the purview of the military technician, and he would be notified of discussions of such matters only insofar as they had military implications.[26] Clemenceau enclosed in his reply to Foch a letter of October 21 from his docile Foreign Affairs Minister, Stephen Pichon, who was even more explicit in assigning Marshal Foch to his sphere. Pichon rejected the request for a liaison officer to inform the marshal of the Quai d'Orsay's plans. Pichon wrote:

It is the Minister of Foreign Affairs who weighs the questions of diplomatic guarantees which he believes ought to be included in the armistice terms as well as in the conditions of peace. He submits these proposals to the government, which makes the decision. The responsibility of the commander-in-chief of the French and Allied Armies is not involved in these matters which are the concern of the government, which will inform him of the measures to be taken. Any other conception of the role of the military authority in working out the clauses of an armistice or peace treaty would create confusion as to responsibilities, and would result in a complicated situation.[27]

Clemenceau, in his version of the incident, stated that he could construe Foch's request for a liaison official with the Quai d'Orsay

---

[26] Clemenceau's letter is quoted in full in Major René Michel Lhopital, *Foch, l'armistice et la paix* (Paris, 1938), pp. 33–36; see also Raymond Recouly, *Le mémorial de Foch: mes entretiens avec le maréchal* (Paris, 1929), p. 45.

[27] Pichon's letter is quoted in full in Lhopital, pp. 36–39; cf. Recouly, p. 43.

only "as an invitation to relinquish in his favor the authority vested in my office." He would never give a second thought to any such abdication, which in any case the Allies would not have allowed since it would have reduced Clemenceau to the role of a diplomatic messenger who merely conveyed the soldier's decisions.[28] Clemenceau assumed that the liaison officer would inform the President of the Council of the marshal's plans, rather than the reverse.

Foch accepted Clemenceau's reproof with philosophical calm but with an unshaken conviction that the statesman was wrong. He thought Clemenceau's notion that "the general ought to work in one sphere and the statesman and diplomat in another . . . not only false but absurd. War, like peace, is not a duality but an integer. It does not call for a military compartment here and a civilian compartment there. The two are closely combined." [29] The marshal's argument is at bottom specious. Obviously soldiers and statesmen must coöperate; it is equally platitudinous and equally important that in deciding basic policy there must be one constituted authority having the last word, and in France—as in most countries—it was the civilian head of the government who was responsible for policy. If Foch had any legitimate grievance during the peace conference, it was Clemenceau's crabbed reluctance to keep him adequately informed of policy under formulation by the government. This Clemenceau could easily have done through direct conversation with the marshal, or through explanations delivered by Foreign Affairs Minister Pichon.

Whatever his private convictions, Foch deferred for the present to the civilian chief. When the marshal called upon Clemenceau on November 11, 1918, he handed him the German armistice papers with a remark of exemplary correctness: "My work is finished; your work begins." [30] This little scene was a model of civil-military punctilio, assigning as it did the technical work of the armistice to

---

[28] Georges Clemenceau, *Grandeur and Misery of Victory* (New York, 1930), pp 260–261. English translation.

[29] Recouly, p. 45.

[30] Charles Bugnet, *Foch Speaks* (New York, 1929), p. 266. English translation.

the soldier and the peace-making role to the statesman, but the drama of Clemenceau and Foch called for the reading of formalized lines which were hard for the headstrong protagonists to deliver at length. The temptation to speak *ad libitum* proved overpowering time and again.

After having ostentatiously put Foch in his place, Clemenceau soon requested him as technician to draw up a memorandum on the very question of bounding Germany at the Rhine.[31] Any inconsistency in this action was only apparent, since the statesman not only had the right but the obligation to ask for technical counsel on so basic a problem in foreign policy. Conferring with a technician is of course a different matter from accepting the technician's dictation—a distinction not always clear to Marshal Foch although understood well enough by Clemenceau. Foch obediently drew up a five-page note, dated November 26, 1918, in which the marshal advanced his conception of the West's strategic security, which he was to repeat indefatigably during the following seven months. It was the familiar plan of cutting off Germany at the Rhine—a bold design already embroidered with many imaginative variations by private French citizens.

The armistice, according to Foch, placed the armies of the Entente in the advantageous position of controlling the Left bank of the Rhine, with bridgeheads upon the Right, from which points they could easily renew the offensive if that should prove necessary. But this provisional advantage should be made permanent by the final determination in the Treaty of Peace of a regime for the Left bank of the Rhine.

To enable France and Western Europe (deprived henceforth of a Russian ally by the Revolution) to stave off a mass of from 64,000,000 to 75,000,000 Volksdeutsche living East of the Rhine, it was necessary to make the river the enemy's western frontier. "Without this fundamental precaution Western Europe would still be deprived of all natural frontiers, and it would lie open to the dangers of an invasion which remained as easy as in the past. But even a

[31] Jean Jules Mordacq, *Le ministère Clemenceau: journal d'un témoin* Paris, 1931), III, 79–80.

frontier as strong as the Rhine with its approaches could be crossed by surprise or by force if it were not held at the outset by sufficient forces, which is to say, by the neighbors of the assailant." Foch estimated the populations of Belgium, Luxembourg, Alsace Lorraine, and France at 49,560,000. Even with the addition of the 5,400,000 residents of the West bank of the Rhine, a total of only 54,960,000 Westerners would confront a German-speaking bloc of from 64,000,-000 to 75,000,000 living East of the river. Therefore it was infeasible to allow any neutral states on the Left bank; the Rhinelanders, although to become citizens of autonomous states, should bear arms in a common defense with the neighboring powers to the West. As a final measure to offset German numerical superiority, it would be vitally necessary "to prepare for the eventual support of the forces of Great Britain, in case of war with the German masses of Central Europe."

Foch concluded his memorandum with the assertion that, while France, Belgium, and England, "with their parliamentary and democratic institutions," renounced any idea of annexation of German soil, they would nevertheless want to maintain the peace by stationing their own contingents along the natural frontier of the Rhine—at least for a specified time; by allowing the organization of autonomous Rhineland states on the West bank; and by retaining the bridgeheads on the East bank as a guarantee of German payment of indemnities and reparations.[32]

In the judgment of André Tardieu, one of the French delegates to the Versailles Conference, this demand that "the German inhabitants of the Left bank of the Rhine be included in the French military establishment" was, in effect, "an extreme proposal amounting to annexation in disguise which had never been endorsed by the French government."[33] That Foch in his heart wanted annexation is highly probable,[34] but in this hope the marshal differed from French statesmen only in considering a massive truncation of Ger-

[32] Terrail, *Le combat des trois,* pp. 205–210.

[33] Tardieu, *The Truth About the Treaty,* p. 194.

[34] On this point, see Basil Henry Liddel Hart, *Foch: The Man of Orleans* (Boston, 1932), p. 410.

many as easily realizable. As already mentioned, there was a wide-spread desire in France for annexation. On this question, according to Gabriel Terrail, "Clemenceau did not think a whit differently from the marshal, from Poincaré, from Briand, from Doumergue, from all Frenchmen" [35]—excepting the Socialists.[36] But in his memoirs Clemenceau drew the distinction between his attitude and Foch's: "I fought to the bitter end for the strategic frontier that Marshal Foch judged to be best, without cherishing any illusions about the internal and external new difficulties." [37] Being the official negotiator and thus in contact with day-to-day reality, Clemenceau could measure the growing strength of the Allied opposition to the Rhineland scheme, while the marshal clung obstinately to his Platonic archetype of strategic security, quite oblivious to all risk of alienating France's urgently needed allies.[38]

The marshal was as hard to discourage as he was to instruct. Had he been as proficient in the intricacies of diplomacy as he imagined, he would have recognized at once those "external difficulties" referred to by Clemenceau. For in a seeming paradox Clemenceau, the jealous guardian of the civilian prerogative, decided to capitalize upon Foch's prestige during a triumphal state visit to London on December 1, 1918. Foch was allowed to present formally France's Rhineland scheme to Prime Minister David Lloyd George, Chancellor of the Exchequer Bonar Law, and General Sir Henry Wilson at a gathering at No. 10 Downing Street. Clemenceau was absent from this important meeting, pleading a "conflicting social engagement." The British Prime Minister at once surmised that his astute French counterpart wanted to draw maximum advantage from the well-known British gratitude toward Foch, who would broach a most touchy question.[39]

---

[35] Terrail, p. 194.

[36] On the Socialist attitude concerning the Rhineland, see Joseph Paul-Boncour, *Entre deux guerres: souvenirs sur la IIIe république* (Paris, 1945), II, 41–43.

[37] Clemenceau, *Grandeur and Misery,* p. 233.

[38] Terrail, pp. 223–224.

[39] David Lloyd George, *The Truth About the Peace Treaties* (London, 1938), I, 132.

Foch advanced all of the main arguments for a Rhine barrier which he had previously set forth in his memorandum of November 26 intended for Clemenceau's instruction. After listening to the marshal's exposition, Lloyd George asked him about the future status of the German provinces on the Left bank of the Rhine. Foch replied cautiously—and vaguely—that "they would probably be independent. They might consist of one state or several states. All that he insisted on was that they should be included in [one] economic and military system. His object was not to annex or to conquer, but merely to provide proper defense against the seventy-five million inhabitants on the Right bank of the Rhine." [40]

When asked how he could reconcile the French proposals with President Wilson's Fourteen Points, Foch replied that the Western Entente was dealing with an aggressor who had disregarded his treaty obligations and whose signature could not be trusted in the future. Hence, it was necessary to have a material guarantee, such as the Rhine barrier. [41] When asked how the Rhinelanders might be induced to consent to such an excision, Foch explained that they could find compelling economic advantages in being on the side of the victors—thereby hinting at a possible remission for them of a war indemnity, as well as profitable trade with the West. As for the danger of creating an Alsace-Lorraine fixation on the German side and consequently incurring the risk of a war of revenge, the marshal contended that precautions (what precautions he did not specify) could be taken "to conciliate the feelings and interests of these people." Bonar Law was not convinced by this line of reasoning, and he pointed out that in the past "Germany had said exactly the same thing. We ourselves had tried for years to conciliate the Irish." [42] Undaunted by the politely skeptical interrogation of the British, the marshal promised to submit to them a written memorandum upon the Rhineland, which he did on January 10, 1919.

Meanwhile the Foreign Affairs Commission of the Chamber of Deputies expressed its approval of a detached Rhineland. On

[40] Lloyd George, I, 134.
[41] Lloyd George, I, 135.
[42] Lloyd George, I, 135; cf. Terrail, p. 195.

December 2, 1918, it drew up the following memorandum for the government's private instruction, which contained a variation of Marshal Foch's scheme:

The Commission, after studying the problem of the French frontier posed by the war, is of the opinion

(1) That there must be demanded the frontier line of 1814 between France and Germany, including the territories of Schaumbourg and Tholey, which until that time had never ceased to belong to France.

(2) That France must demand in the territories between the line of 1814 and the Dutch frontier a number of military, economic and political guarantees (especially in regard to railways, canals and customs) which, although excluding any idea of annexation, will nevertheless free this region from Prussian influence and protect our country from invasion.

Especially must there be no troops nor military establishment, nor fortifications on the Left bank of the Rhine; the same should apply to a thirty kilometer zone on the Right bank. The inhabitants of the Left bank will in no case be compelled to perform military service.

(3) Moreover, as regards the Rhine, a policy of internationalization of the river, under the President of France, entails a revision of the Gothard convention.

(4) As regards Luxembourg, which must be free to decide its destiny, France will respect the will of its inhabitants expressed in a regular plebiscite.

In summary, the Commission believes that the conditions of a just and durable peace for France could be reduced to three points:

(1) Total reimbursement of war costs and reparation for direct damages caused persons and property.

(2) The retrocession to France of the frontiers of 1814 including the entire Saar basin.

(3) Military, political and economic guarantees of the territories of the Left bank of the Rhine which would definitely protect France from invasion.

These measures, like all the others of the Treaty of Peace, will acquire new and decisive value from the creation of a League of Nations, to the principles of which the Foreign Affairs Commission fully adheres.[43]

---

[43] Quoted by Senator Léon Bourgeois in *Annales du Sénat, documents parlementaires* . . . Séance du 3 octobre 1919, p. 586. See also Vial-Mazel,

This memorandum differed from Foch's scheme in that it envisaged the internationalization of the Rhine under the supervision of the French President. The marshal wanted to create autonomous states on the Left bank, but with the requirement that the citizens of such states should bear arms in a common defense with the Western powers. The Foreign Affairs Commission was determined that the Rhinelanders should remain disarmed. Both schemes were at bottom plans for the indirect control of the Rhineland from Paris rather than from Berlin. Of the two, the plan of the Foreign Affairs Commission was the more implausible, since it would have been hard to take seriously the independence of an "internationalized" Rhineland under the aegis of the French President. Everyone would have recognized such a regime as disguised annexation by Paris, which the British would not have accepted in any case.

But Marshal Foch's Rhineland project was almost as infeasible, since it must be emphasized that the ingenious scheme presupposed British participation to offset the preponderance of perhaps as many as 75,000,000 Volksdeutsche East of the Rhine, over the 55,000,000 Western Europeans (not counting the British, but including—optimistically—the estimated 5,400,000 Rhinelander allies). To excise Germany so provocatively while leaving 75,000,000 predictable advocates of revenge in the unoccupied regions east of the Rhine—to do all this without a binding guarantee of British support—was to sow the whirlwind. According to Foch's own argument, merely holding the river and its approaches would not in itself be an adequate safeguard: sufficient Allied troops would have to man a new *limes Germanicus* until Germany had paid off all its obligations. Yet the British had already stated that they would not agree to a detached Rhineland. As far back as December 19, 1917, soon after the Bolsheviks had divulged the contents of the secret treaties, Arthur Balfour, the British Foreign Secretary, had said to the House of Commons in reference to the Pokrovsky-Doumergue Rhineland agreement: "It is pure fancy. . . . Never, at any moment, has such a scheme formed

---

Erreurs et oublis de Georges Clemenceau, pp. 206–208; and Edward M. House and Charles Seymour, eds., *What Really Happened at Paris* (New York, 1921), p. 52.

part of the policy of His Majesty's Government. The Government has never been aware that any such scheme was seriously considered by any French politician." [44] Nevertheless Foch seemed to be assuming that the merits of the Rhineland scheme were as luminously self-evident to the British as to the French.

In retrospect, one might inquire why Foch did not advocate the total occupation and disarmament of Germany, as Soviet Russia, the United States, Britain, and France were to do in 1945. As the war drew to a close in the autumn of 1918, Foch had steadfastly opposed the idea of total occupation. When questioned by Clemenceau about the proposals of President Poincaré[45] and of the American Generals John J. Pershing[46] and Tasker H. Bliss,[47] to fight all the way to Berlin, Foch had replied: "To continue the struggle longer would incur great risk. It would mean that perhaps fifty or a hundred thousand more Frenchmen would be killed, not counting the Allies, and for quite problematic results. . . . Enough blood, alas! has already been shed and that should suffice." [48] Clemenceau had expressed full agreement with this opinion.[49] Foch also minimized the importance of disarming Germany. When questioned about this possible guarantee, Foch had said: "Disarmament, one cannot repeat too often, gives us only a temporary, precarious, fictitious security. It is almost impossible to prevent Germany from arming in secret. . . . If [Germany] has the will to wage war, nothing will prevent it from finding the means and nothing proves that these means will not be effective. . . . Weakness, more or less pretended, in your adversary does not create strength in you." [50] Foch, then, had adopted

[44] Quoted in Tardieu, *The Truth About the Treaty*, p. 367; cf. article by Tardieu in *Le Temps*, September 13, 1921; and Lloyd George, *The Truth*, I, 384–385.

[45] Gordon Wright, *Raymond Poincaré and the French Presidency* (Stanford University, Cal., 1942), p. 182.

[46] Harry R. Rudin, *Armistice 1918* (New Haven, Conn., 1944), p. 186.

[47] Rudin, p. 183.

[48] Jean Jules Mordacq, *La verité sur l'armistice* (Paris, 1929), p. 58.

[49] Clemenceau, *Grandeur and Misery*, p. 114.

[50] Recouly, *Le mémorial de Foch*, pp. 242–243; cf. Raymond Recouly, *La barrière du Rhin* (Paris, 1923), pp. 8–9.

the questionable position of opposing the total occupation and disarmament of the enemy, and yet he advocated a massive truncation
of the Rhineland which would not have crushed Germany, but which
would have been certain to produce a perpetual irredendist agitation. This was an even more doubtful guarantee of peace, especially
when the indispensable ally, Britain, refused to acquiesce in the
scheme.

The United States government was equally opposed to the French
Rhineland project, although its representatives were slower to reveal
their disapproval. President Wilson's emissary, Colonel Edward M.
House, fomented French hopes during the armistice discussions in
October 1918 by his sympathetic support of their proposal to station
occupation forces temporarily on both banks of the Rhine. American
complaisance in this question was in contrast to the British opposition
to the occupation of the East bank, which Lloyd George pronounced
"unwise." [51] Misleading the French further in their expectation of
continuing American support was Colonel House's willingness to
maintain the Rhineland occupation until the treaty obligations were
fulfilled, the German army reduced to 150,000, and the League of
Nations organized. Sufficient attention was not given to the fact
that this meant an occupation of only limited duration; it certainly
did not mean creating a separate political Rhineland entity.[52] For
the avoidance of misunderstanding, it was unfortunate that Marshal
Foch did not know of a conversation which Colonel House had
with British Foreign Secretary Arthur Balfour on February 9, 1919,
which the American representative reported as follows:

We talked at great length of the French proposal of setting up a
"Rhenish Republic" as a buffer state between Germany and France. The
French have but one idea and that is military protection. They do not
seem to know that to establish a Rhenish Republic against the will of
the people would be contrary to the principle of self-determination and
that if we establish it, the people could at any time become federated with

[51] Charles Seymour, ed., *The Intimate Papers of Colonel House* (New
York, 1928), IV, 118.
[52] Seymour, *Colonel House*, IV, 344–346; cf. Lloyd George, *The Truth*,
I, 398–399.

the other German states. If we did such a thing, we would be treating Germany in one way and the balance of the world in another.[53]

American reticence nurtured French illusions to the point that they were ill-prepared for the discouraging instructions eventually cabled to Colonel House by President Wilson on March 10: "I hope you will not even provisionally consent to the separation of the Rhenish provinces from Germany under any arrangement, but will reserve the whole matter until my arrival." [54]

In fulfillment of his promise given in London on December 1, 1918, Marshal Foch drew up a second Rhineland memorandum which he addressed to the Commanders-in-Chief of the Allied armies on January 10, 1919. The marshal began the paper with a historical account of the rise of militarism in Germany, and of the repeated use of the Rhineland as a springboard for invasion of the West. Again Foch advanced the thesis that "henceforth the Rhine should be the *military* western frontier of the German peoples." [55] But the broad hint of disguised annexation of the Rhineland contained in the note of November 26, 1918 was now superseded by a demand for the occupation of the Left bank, with the encouragement there of new autonomous states, governing themselves, although joined by a customs union to the other Western European states.[56]

Lloyd George, upon receiving his copy of the promised memorandum, made an observation which was portentous for the French proposal: "On my last trip to Paris my strongest impression was the statue of Strasbourg in its veil of mourning. Do not allow Germany to erect such a statue." [57]

Foch was assiduously propagandizing his scheme at the time the Peace Conference was supposed to convene. Clemenceau, on January 8, 1919, had issued a decree naming the French plenipotentiaries to the Peace Conference: the Tiger himself ex officio as the President

[53] Seymour, IV, 345.

[54] Seymour, IV, 345; cf. Charles Homer Haskins, "The New Boundaries of Germany," in House and Seymour, eds., *What Really Happened at Paris,* p. 52.

[55] Italics mine.

[56] Terrail, *Le combat des trois,* pp. 210–217.

[57] Mordacq, *Le ministère Clemenceau,* III, 80 n.

of the Council, Stephen Pichon, André Tardieu, Louis L. Klotz, and Jules Cambon.[58] Marshal Foch was sixth on the list, but since the delegation of each of the Great Powers was limited to five, the title of plenipotentiary was given to the soldier only as a courtesy.[59] The marshal nevertheless wanted to address the opening session of the conference, but he was told by Foreign Affairs Minister Pichon not to attend.[60] This refusal greatly irritated Foch. The director of the press bureau of the American Peace Commission, Ray Stannard Baker, witnessed a scene between the marshal and Foreign Minister Pichon which revealed the mounting tension between Foch and his government. As Baker described it:

One morning—this was in January not long after the beginning of the conference—I saw [Foreign Minister Pichon's] doors burst suddenly open . . . and out strode a short, stocky, gray-haired man, very erect, who looked like some old and studious college professor, but who wore the uniform of a marshal of France. Behind him came flying the little, agile Pichon, pleading with him to return.

"Jamais, jamais!" said Marshal Foch angrily.

No, he would never return. . . . But in a moment he was suddenly persuaded; and he did go back, and the . . . doors closed again behind him.[61]

Foch was not really mollified over his exclusion from the conference. Conveniently disregarding his fruitless parley with Lloyd George and Bonar Law on December 1, 1918, Foch told his friend Raymond Recouly that he found it difficult to understand why Clemenceau did not use him to support the French thesis to overcome the resistance of the others. Foch contended that Clemenceau could have said to them:

"I am obliged to listen to Foch in all matters of security. Now Foch will not hear any solution except the military frontier of the Rhine. Anything you could offer us in exchange, the disarmament of Germany, a treaty of alliance, temporary occupation, appears absolutely insufficient

[58] Mordacq, III, 76.
[59] Terrail, p. 204.
[60] Recouly, *Le mémorial de Foch,* p. 188.
[61] Baker, *Woodrow Wilson and World Settlement,* I, 163.

to him. . . ." I cannot understand the spirit which possessed [Clemenceau]. Was he jealous of the military? Fearful of seeing a general mix in diplomatic negotiations, desirous of affirming civilian supremacy? In so grave a matter it is not a question of soldiers and civilians, but solely of the broad interests of the country, in the protection of which all should work shoulder to shoulder.[62]

As for this complaint, Liddell Hart observed that it was unlikely that Foch would have made more of an impression on the Allied statesmen with greater opportunity for addressing them. He was actually to have many such opportunities and the effect was only to crystallize opposition, especially from Lloyd George and President Wilson, neither of whom wanted to tolerate military intervention in discussions of policy.[63] Lloyd George stated his views quite explicitly on this subject at one of the sessions of the Big Four: "The concurrence [of the military] is essential in time of war. But in the domain of the statesman, they are the last ones I would consult. I admire and love Marshal Foch very much, but on political questions he is an infant. I would not take his advice as to the means of assuring nations the most effective security." [64]

Foch failed utterly to appreciate the diplomatic difficulties confronting the French government in its negotiations with its allies. He gave no credit to Clemenceau for his use of patience, personal persuasion, and the soft tone in trying to win over Lloyd George and Wilson to the acceptance of the French Rhineland project. The fiery soldier seemed to want to sound a bugle and to strike dumb France's carping critics.[65] General Mordacq, the Tiger's military adviser, related an anecdote concerning Foch's incomprehension. Mordacq wrote that on February 2, 1919, at a meeting of Foch, Pichon, Louis Loucheur, and André Tardieu with Clemenceau, the marshal, recalling his numerous altercations with the Tiger over his alleged laxness in commanding the American army, said upon entering

[62] Recouly, pp. 188–190.
[63] Liddell Hart, *Foch*, p. 413.
[64] Paul Mantoux, ed., *Les délibérations du conseil des quatre* (Paris, 1955), I, 46.
[65] On this point, see Recouly, pp. 190–193.

Clemenceau's office: "Well, Mister President, I see that now that you have to lead the Allies, you discover as I did that it is not always easy." To which the President of the Council replied: "Pardon, Marshal. You have forgotten one thing: you were their chief and were recognized as such. You therefore could order them. With me it is an altogether different matter. I have no authority to give them orders." [66]

In contrast to Foch, Lloyd George was appreciative of Clemenceau's patience and subtlety as a negotiator. The British Prime Minister observed that it was significant that Clemenceau did not bring up the thorny Rhineland question at the official meetings of the Peace Conference. He was careful to avoid the bad psychology of the inevitable rebuffs. Instead the wily old French politician sought out members of the British and American delegations, and in separate, personal conversations he tirelessly reiterated the French demand for a Rhine frontier as a guarantee of peace.[67]

[66] Mordacq, *Le ministère Clemenceau*, III, 109–110.

[67] See report of P. W. Slosson, "Documentary History of the Treaty of Peace Between the Allied and Associated Powers and Germany," Part III, Section III, p. 2, in the Henry White Papers, 1919, Library of Congress, Washington, D.C.; cf. Lloyd George, *The Truth*, I, 386.

Chapter II

Separatist Reveries

Events in Germany, meanwhile, lent some encouragement to Foch and to the other proponents of Rhineland separatism. In the last weeks of the war, in October 1918, a group of Cologne Rhinelanders, seeing the handwriting on the wall for Germany, organized a Committee for a Free Rhine under the leadership of Bertram Kastert, the vicar of Sainte-Colomba and a Reichstag Deputy.[1] The objective of this committee was to bring about a completely independent Rhenish state, freed not only from Prussian but also from German control. Kastert soon found a rival in the Catholic Centrist politician, Charles Trimborn, Under-Secretary of State in Berlin and an aspirant to the future presidency of the Rhineland state.[2] Trimborn counseled against Kastert's plan of proclaiming forthwith an independent Rhineland state, advancing instead the more cautious slogan: "a Free Rhineland in a Free Germany."[3] Trimborn wanted to avoid a clean break with Germany, preferring some sort of federal tie with Berlin.

Schism hampered the separatist movement at the time of the overthrow of the Hohenzollern monarchy. Moreover, the Social Democratic Deputy of Cologne, the Prussian Wilhelm Sollman, stole a march on the other separatist factions by setting up in

---

[1] [Hans] A. Dorten, *La tragédie rhénane* (Paris, 1945), p. 36.

[2] Fritz Brüggemann, *Die Rheinische Republik* (Bonn, 1919), pp. 11–12.

[3] Rhineland Republic, Vorlaeufige Regierung der Rheinischen Republik zu Wiesbaden. *Die Rheinische Republik: Die Gruende fuer die Errichtung eines Rheinischen Freistaates und die Vorgeschichte der Proklamation vom. 1. Juni 1919* (Wiesbaden, 1919), pp. 3–4. Hereafter cited as *Die Gruende.*

November 1918 an ephemeral Workers and Soldiers Council in the Rhenish city.[4] Another setback to inchoate separatism occurred when the French government, determined upon a German policy of multilateral guarantees, announced that the Rhineland would be divided into four zones of military occupation. The Belgians would be stationed in Aachen, the British in Cologne, the Americans in Coblenz, and the French in Mainz.[5] Anglo-American presence would greatly hinder the separatists, since the French alone were seriously regarded as favoring the movement.

The militant Bertram Kastert felt that he would have to confront the hostile British with an accomplished fact upon their arrival in Cologne, so he convoked a so-called "Constituent Assembly of the Free State of the Free Rhine" on December 4, 1918. But at the meeting in the Gürzenich Hall attended by several thousand Rhinelanders, the Trimborn faction obstructed all attempts by Kastert to proclaim at once the independence of the Rhineland. Trimborn dominated the proceedings and obtained the passage of a resolution urging "the official representatives of the Rhenish and Westphalian people to proclaim as soon as possible the founding of an autonomous Rhenish-Westphalian republic within the framework of Germany."[6] Those separatists who wanted a clean break with Germany were convinced that Trimborn's supporters among the Centrists and land owners were counting upon their recognized numerical strength in Western Germany to enable them to dominate any future Rhenish political entity. The Centrists, meanwhile, wanted assurances of Allied military and political protection before challenging Prussian control of the Rhineland.[7]

The effective leadership of the Rhenish separatist movement soon devolved upon an obscure figure, Dr. Hans Adam Dorten, a native of Endenich and a former public prosecutor of Düsseldorf who had fought in the war as a captain in command of a group of anti-

---

[4] Dorten, p. 38; cf. Brüggemann, pp. 19–20.

[5] Dorten, p. 36.

[6] *Die Gruende,* p. 6; Joseph Aulneau, *Le Rhin et la France* (Paris, 1921), p. 219.

[7] Dorten, p. 39.

aircraft batteries on the Verdun front.[8] Dorten was described by
Guy de Traversay as the possessor of "much opportunism but also
of profound conviction. Of cosmopolitan taste and British in appearance, he was more French in inclinations. He was gifted in
culture and history, but, alas, he had little sense of economic
reality." [9] Dorten was nonetheless a member of the Rhineland
Industrialists Club. At Düsseldorf, in December 1918, he met with
half a dozen industrialists who criticized the indecision of the
Trimborn faction of Centrists. The magnates stressed the importance
to industry of the Rhineland movement, which could have decisive
consequences for the economic life of the region. "We are convinced," they told Dorten,

. . . that victorious France will annex the Left bank of the Rhine, while
the regions on the other bank will become a prey of Bolshevism. Thus
part of us will be delivered to the good will of the French; the rest will
be at the mercy of the Spartacists. To avoid this pitfall, it is vitally
necessary to avoid the separation of the two banks of the Rhine. What
is to be done . . . ? There remains oony one possibility: the creation of an
independent Rhineland state, including almost all of the industrial
regions on the two banks of the Rhine. Once set up, such a state would
allow us to confer directly with the victors and it would serve as a basis
of close collaboration with France, whose economy corresponds best to
our needs.[10]

The industrialists requested Dorten to "give momentum to the
Rhineland movement which languished in the hands of the Centrist
leaders," with whom he was to begin negotiations. Dorten was also
to establish relations with the French occupying authorities.[11]

The French forces of occupation in Germany were under two field
commanders. General Charles Mangin, commanding the Tenth
Army with headquarters at Mainz, controlled parts of Hesse and
Rhenish Prussia; General Augustin Gérard, commanding the Eighth
Army with headquarters at Landau, controlled all of the Palatinate.

---

[8] *Kölnische Zeitung,* June 4, 1919; cf. Brüggemann, p. 117.

[9] Guy de Traversay, "La première tentative de République rhénane," *La
Revue de Paris* (15 November 1928), p. 425.

[10] Dorten, pp. 40–41.

[11] Dorten, p. 41.

No love was lost between these two antipathetic French generals. Gérard was an unspectacular soldier but a militant freemason and an ardent republican. Mangin, a conservative, was renowned as the colonial officer who had helped Marchand implant the tricolor at Fashoda in 1898, and more recently he had been acclaimed as the conqueror of Forts Vaux and Douaumont. The two did not attempt any coöordination in abetting separatism. Above these two field commanders was General Emile Fayolle who commanded an army group. Fayolle had no taste for politics, leaving such matters largely up to Mangin and Gérard.[12] Marshal Foch soon transferred his own headquarters from Luxembourg to Kreuznach to be near the scene of the Rhenish separatist movement.

Mangin and Gérard—not to mention Marshal Foch himself—wanted first of all to find out precisely what Paris sought in the Rhineland: annexation, one large buffer state, or several small ones. No directive had been received from Clemenceau, who appeared engrossed in his negotiations with the British and Americans. It was March 1919 before General Mangin had the first opportunity of discussing Rhineland policy with Clemenceau.[13] A severe critic of Clemenceau, Georges Vial-Mazel, contended that during the prolonged armistice about the only policy guide available to the French occupation authorities was the vague intimation of possible Rhenish autonomy which could be read into one of President Wilson's precepts: "All territorial settlements ought to be made in the interests of the populations concerned, and not as part of an arrangement or as a compromise of the demands of rival states." The French Ministry of Foreign Affairs did vouchsafe to send to Generals Mangin and Gérard the following ambiguous note: "Make known to the Rhineland populations that the prosperity of their country does not necessarily depend on political ties with the Right bank, and that the decision which will be taken in their regard will not run counter to their own interests." [14] This larvated instruction implied that Paris opposed an independent Rhenish state astride the Rhine; by confin-

---

[12] Traversay, "La première tentative," pp. 423–424.

[13] General Charles Mangin, "Lettres de Rhénanie," *La Revue de Paris* (April 1, 1936), p. 502.

[14] Vial-Mazel, *Erreurs et oublis de Georges Clemenceau*, p. 75.

ing all plans to the Left bank the possibility of future annexation
by France would be kept open. With such a directive, the French
occupation authorities were naturally reserved when they were first
approached by Rhenish separatists with grandiose plans for a large
Rhineland republic on both banks of the river. Vial-Mazel added
the wry observation that if the occupation authorities enjoyed a
certain freedom of initiative, it was because they were without
instructions from the government.[15]

Slowly emerging as the principal Centrist leader in the Rhineland
was Konrad Adenauer, the Mayor of Cologne, who was to toy with
separatism. Supple and cautious, Adenauer sounded out first a
French officer who visited Cologne, but he could learn nothing from
him as to the French Rhineland intentions. The mayor thereupon
approached the British who seemed more responsive to his overtures.
The Chief of the Political Department of British headquarters in
Cologne, Lieutenant-Colonel Rupert S. Ryan, apparently acting on
his own authority, encouraged Adenauer to lead a movement which
might come under British influence, for there were to be no changes
in the status quo without British agreement. Adenauer felt that a
quasi-legal means was essential for realizing separatist aspirations.
He proposed to the leaders of local committees that the separatists
take part in the forthcoming electoral campaigns for the German
Constituent Assembly as well as the Prussian Constituent Assembly.
Any candidate receiving separatist support would have to take an
oath in favor of an independent Rhineland. After the balloting, the
separatists would compel their deputies (legally elected to the
German and Prussian Constituent Assemblies) not to leave for
Berlin but to remain behind to participate in an *ad hoc* Rhineland
Constituent Assembly, which would be convoked immediately. This
would give at least a semblance of legality to a new Rhenish state,
so Adenauer reasoned. It seemed plausible, since three-fourths of the
Rhineland deputies were ordinarily Centrists, and the Center, following the lead of Kastert, Trimborn, and now Adenauer, favored
a special status for its Rhineland stronghold.[16]

[15] Vial-Mazel, pp. 77–78; cf. General Charles Mangin, p. 484.
[16] See report of Captain H. E. Osann to Assistant Chief of Staff G2, in

When Dr. Dorten, in compliance with the request of the Rhine-land Industrialists Club, went to parley with Konrad Adenauer in December 1918, he was cordially received. Adenauer told Dorten that the British were opposed to the creation of a Rhenish state which would embrace the entire Rhineland, since such an entity would eventually fall a prey to French domination. However, Adenauer believed that the British might accept a much smaller West German free state in their own zone of occupation. Dorten expressed opposition to the fracturing of the new Rhenish state, for it was apparent that if a state were set up in the British zone, the French would counter with one in their zone. "If you want to avoid such an unfortunate division," Adenauer replied, "there are two conditions to be met: give me the adherence of the South, and assure me of the consent, or better still, of the effective support of the French." [17] This implied that two Rhenish states might in future be joined, despite British opposition. Adenauer appeared ready to proceed without the consent of the German or Prussian governments. He was receptive to the idea of including in the new Rhenish state territory on the East bank of the Rhine, paralleling the river, and extending as far as the Rothaargebirge. According to Dorten, when Adenauer was questioned as to whether the new state would remain within the framework of the Reich, he replied that the question would be broached at an opportune time.[18]

In a letter to me dated September 5, 1956, Adenauer declared that he never favored separation from Germany: "From the very beginning I opposed the separation of the Rhineland from Germany, and I said that to Dr. Dorten so clearly and firmly that I did not receive him after 1 February." [19] [the date of the convocation of the Cologne Constituent Assembly]. Adenauer was probably suffering from

---

the Tasker H. Bliss Papers, 1919, Library of Congress, Washington, D.C.; cf. *Die Gruende,* pp. 35–36; cf. also Brüggemann, *Die Rheinische Republik,* pp. 17–20, 24–25.

[17] Dorten, *La tragédie rhénane,* p. 45.

[18] Dorten, p. 45.

[19] Letter from Konrad Adenauer to me, 5 September 1956; see also Paul Binoux, *La question rhénane et la France* (Paris, 1946), p. 89.

selective amnesia when questioned about this ticklish subject thirty-seven years after the event, at a time when any acknowledgment of having once been a separatist would be a political liability in the divided Germany of today. Dorten's memory (the tenacious recollection of a man who never knew political success) is the more credible, since separatism was to be his life's work, and not a mere momentary indiscretion, as in Adenauer's case.

Dorten promised to concern himself with the American and French zones of occupation, south of the river Ahr. He would speak with the Hessian and Nassauian Centrist leaders, inviting the mayors of the occupied towns and cities to act in concert with him. He would seek to obtain in the unoccupied regions of Rhenish Hesse and old Nassau "full power to transmit their adherence to the constitution of the Rhenish state." The South, in the person of Dr. Dorten, would thus participate in an *ad hoc* Constituent Assembly of Cologne, and in the foreseeable future there could be created a state comprising the entire Rhineland.[20]

Losing no time, Dorten organized the Hesse-Nassau Committee at Wiesbaden and Mainz, and the Mid-Rhine Committee at Bingen and Kreuznach. The Centrist leaders of these regions fully supported the Adenauer program. In the unoccupied region, Monsignor Hoehler, vicar general of the Bishop of Limburg, collected a number of declarations proclaiming the adherence of municipal councils of Nassau to the Rhineland movement and naming Dorten as their proxy at the special Constituent Asembly to be convoked at Cologne. Dorten was able to bring encouraging news to Adenauer on his second visit to Cologne in December 1918.

But Dorten's first contact with the French occupation authorities was a rebuff. He visited Colonel Pinot, the chief French administrator of the district of Wiesbaden, to explain the Rhineland program. "They do not give a damn for your movement in Paris," the colonel told him bluntly. "There is no point in my importuning general headquarters; therefore, do you really wish to continue?" The following day the Wiesbaden newspapers carried on their first page an official French communiqué, signed by the administrator,

[20] Dorten, *La tragédie rhénane*, p. 46.

declaring that the French Republic would not allow "the creation of a priestly state on the Rhine." [21] Colonel Pinot obviously did not want the separatist movement to preclude French annexation.

Dorten took a patient and long-suffering attitude toward the French. He noted the contradictions in French Rhineland intentions as revealed in the Paris press and in conversations with occupation officials. Some Frenchmen demanded pure and simple annexation of the Left bank of the Rhine; others urged a buffer state; still others wanted the complete abandonment of all Rhineland plans in view of the advantage of large reparations which could be levied upon a unified and centralized Germany. Dorten, as well as Adenauer, was well aware of the British opposition to French annexation of the Rhineland. But both separatist leaders were fully convinced that France could never abandon the intention of remaining on the Rhine. They were confident that Paris would declare in their favor "shortly after the Rhineland problem had been clearly posed"—that is, after the accomplished fact of the creation of an independent, or at least autonomous, Rhineland.[22] Dorten was later to regret that he could not gain access to General Mangin before April 1919, on the assumption that he would have received vitally needed support from this sympathetic figure while the Rhineland situation was more malleable.

Refusing to be daunted by initial setbacks, Dorten visited Adenauer again in the middle of January 1919, eliciting from the mayor the promise that at the February 1 meeting of the Constituent Assembly in Cologne there would be proclaimed the Westdeutscher Freistaat, as planned.[23] Dorten would then announce the adherence of the South, thereby creating a single, large Rhenish state.

Before this plan could be realized, more obstructions were encountered. The German provisional government of Philipp Scheidemann in Berlin got wind of the proposed Cologne convocation of

[21] Adam Dorten, "Le général Mangin en Rhénanie," *Revue des Deux Mondes* (July 1, 1937), p. 40.

[22] Dorten, *La tragédie rhénane,* p. 50.

[23] Dorten, *La tragédie rhénane,* p. 51; cf. Paul Weymar, *Konrad Adenauer* (München, 1955), pp. 71–73.

Rhineland deputies and mayors. The Majority Socialists and other non-Centrists who had been fitfully supporting the Rhineland movement showed signs of wavering. Wilhelm Sollmann began a campaign against it. The Democratic leader, Bernhard Falk, likewise abandoned the movement. The provisional government in Berlin circulated the rumor that the draft of the future German constitution would contain a clause allowing the Rhineland to demand separation from Prussia for the purpose of forming an autonomous state within the German Reich. Taken at face value, this astute gambit seemed to obviate the necessity for the movement led by Adenauer and Dorten. Moreover, if an independent Rhineland state were precipitately proclaimed before receiving international guarantees, it could easily play into the hands of French annexationists, which no German or even Rhenish patriot would desire.[24]

Adenauer was disturbed by these considerations. The mayor of Cologne was becoming suspicious of the British as well as the French. He learned from the Political Department of the British occupation forces in Cologne that at the Peace Conference in Paris the British were opposing Rhenish independence. They were winning President Wilson's support in trying to convince the French that they should abandon their Rhineland demands in exchange for a system of collective security which would be underwritten by an Anglo-American military guarantee.[25]

On February 1, just before the convocation of the Rhineland Constituent Assembly, Adenauer was not amused by the reported finding of a newly dug grave bearing the epitaph: "Here lies Konrad Adenauer, first President of the Rhineland Republic." The mayor needed no such crude reminder of the advantages of caution in his proposals to the *ad hoc* Assembly. While Dorten awaited the promised proclamation of the Westdeutscher Freistaat to which he would offer the South's adherence, Adenauer was seeking a double-hinged formula which would keep open the door both for Rhenish independence and for escape if necessary. After much debate the special

---

[24] Dorten, *La tragédie rhénane,* p. 52.
[25] Dorten, *La tragédie rhénane,* p. 53.

Rhineland Constituent Assembly accepted Adenauer's proposed resolution: "The dismemberment of Prussia being seriously considered, we authorize the commission named by us to continue the preparation of a West German Republic within the framework of the Reich, on the basis of a constitution to be drafted by the German National Assembly."[26] In 1956 Adenauer defended this formula in the following words: "The purpose of the meeting of February 1 was to gain control over the efforts aiming at a separation from Germany which were made intermittently in the Rhine Province. I was always in favor of a separation from Prussia, and of the formation of a federal Rhineland state within the framework of the German Reich."[27]

The ambiguous text of the Rhineland Constituent Assembly's resolution was designed to please all factions. The separatists could nurture the attenuated hope that a commission of nine members might try to do what Adenauer and most of the delegates of the Constituent Assembly were reluctant to do—actually proclaim a West German republic. But the commission could act only in conformity with the German National Assembly which was at work in Weimar framing a new German constitution. A free Rhineland would thus have to be supported by a majority of the members of the German National Assembly—a most unlikely prospect.[28]

Dorten was irritated with Adenauer's "tergiversations." He claimed that on February 2 he visited the mayor and urged the immediate convocation of the commission which was to be made up of representatives of the principal political parties. Dorten considered the presence of three Prussians on the commission a virtual guarantee of faineance on its part, although Adenauer pretended to be nonetheless confident of the outcome of the commission's work. Dorten contended that Adenauer exhorted him to go on with his efforts

[26] *Kölnische Volkszeitung,* February 2, 1919; cf. Dorten, *La tragédie rhénane,* p. 54; Weymar, *Konrad Adenauer,* p. 74.

[27] Letter from Konrad Adenauer to me, 5 September 1956; cf. Brüggemann, *Die Rheinische Republik,* pp. 46–51; see also Weymar, p. 79.

[28] Traversay, "La première tentative de République rhénane," p. 426.

in the South—especially with the French authorities—in behalf of an independent Rhineland. Now, however, he distrusted Adenauer's sincerity, all the more so when the month of February passed without any sign of activity in Cologne and without the commission ever being convened.[29] Dorten decided to pursue an independent course, following his own initiative with the Rhineland committees of the South.

Beyond Dorten's chosen bailiwick, at Landau in the Bavarian Palatinate, in General Gérard's zone of occupation, a variant of separatism came to the surface quite independently of Dorten's movement. A self-constituted assembly of forty-five "notables" gathered at the Hotel Schwan to discuss the Bolshevik menace and the disorders roiling life in Berlin and Munich. They listened to an address from Hermann Hofmann, the President of the Bavarian Popular Party, and a Deputy to the German Constituent Assembly, as well as a separatist. Hofmann described the "chaos" in Berlin, a city which lay under the Spartacist shadow. He acknowledged loyalty not to Bavaria but to Germany, and he denied that the Palatinate had ever had militarist sentiments. He insisted that it was not high treason but solicitude for "our little country" which prompted the residents of the Palatinate to place themselves under the protection of "the nations which have emerged victorious from the war." [30]

At the close of the meeting the group passed a resolution which was to be forwarded to the Peace Conference at Versailles by General Gérard. It read as follows:

A large number of the residents of the Palatinate wish to see created an autonomous Republic of the Palatinate. Proponents of this idea are convinced that this plan could be realized only in agreement with the Peace Conference.

Relying upon the principle of self-determination of peoples, they request Monsieur le général commanding the Army of the Palatinate

[29] Dorten, *La tragédie rhénane,* p. 55.

[30] Georges Vial-Mazel, *Le Rhin: victoire allemande* (Paris, 1921), p. 36; cf. Robert Oberhauser, *Kampf der Westmarck* (Neustadt an der Haardt, 1934), pp. 39–40.

to transmit this wish to the Peace Conference. The way in which this idea can be carried out depends upon the advice given by the conference.[31]

When General Gérard duly forwarded this letter to Foch, the marshal said in response that before long the residents of the Palatinate could speak openly for the autonomy which they desired, and they would be safeguarded against any punitive return of the authorities of the Bavarian and German governments.[32] The marshal was understandably delighted over any manifestation of separatism in West Germany, but to what degree was he a captive of wishful fantasy? He may have been indulging in as much of a reverie as the French writer Joesph Aulneau who leaped to the conclusion that the Landau meeting was a separatist ground swell, since the "Palatine notables represented 209,000 votes, or two-thirds of the electors of the Palatinate." [33]

How much popular sentiment was there for independence in the Palatinate, Hesse, Nassau, Rhenish Prussia, and Westphalia? Since there was no official plebiscite on separatism, this question can never be precisely answered. Dr. Dorten attached great importance to a file of declarations and attestations which he collected in the course of his separatist propaganda activities, and which he later deposited with the Hoover Institution on War, Revolution and Peace at Stanford University.[34] A thorough examination of the Dorten Papers does not answer the question as to the strength of separatism in 1919. The Hoover Institution collection includes attestations from seventeen Rhenish mayors, forty-two pastors, and twenty-eight miscellaneous minor dignitaries such as publishers, directors of peasant unions, and the directors of the Social Democratic Party of the Palatinate and of the Nassau Center Party. Thoroughly typical

---

[31] Bavaria, Staatskommissar für die Pfalz. *Die Pfalz unter französischer Besetzung 1918–1924* (München, 1925), p. 14.

[32] *Die Pfalz*, p. 14; cf. Paul Jacquot, *General Gérard und die Pfalz* (Berlin, 1920), pp. 66–67.

[33] Aulneau, *Le Rhin et la France*, p. 227; cf. Clemenceau, *Grandeur and Misery*, pp. 210–211.

[34] Dorten, "Le général Mangin en Rhénanie," p. 41.

of the depositions was the declaration of the pastor of Nieder Laue-
heim: "The majority of the people of this place want a plebiscite to
bring about a Rhenish Republic within the framework of the
German Reich." [35] Even three volumes of such attestations add up
to no more than the hopes of self-constituted members of a pressure-
group; by no stretch of the imagination or semantics could they be
called a poll.

That there were numerous separatists in West Germany in early
1919 is beyond dispute. But their proportion to the total population,
the vehemence of their desire to be independent of Prussia and
Bavaria, their willingness to incur risks for the separatist movement
are all open to doubt. It is equally hard to determine whether the
separatists were chiefly interested in protection from Spartacism;
from Prussian militarism and bureaucracy or absentee Bavarian
rule; from the payment of a war indemnity; or from the eclipsing
of Rhineland Catholics in a Reich two-thirds Protestant. Impossible
to determine is the degree of sheer opportunism among the separatists, some of whom undoubtedly hoped to curry favor with the
victors and obtain office or preferment. Who could assess the basic
motives of Dorten, of Adenauer? The separatist goals were even
more amorphous than those of the French expansionists. Suffice it
to say that Rhineland separatism was at least in part a revival of
particularism in an age of nationalism. This lesser regional loyalty
had no long-run prospect of victory when pitted against the fetish
of German nationalism. There was a contrived quality, an attribute
of self-conscious archaism in the whole movement which foredoomed
it quite as much as British and American opposition to the French
schemes and to Dorten's dreams. But the schemes and illusions were
slow to evaporate.

Dorten and Bertram Kastert, thoroughly suspicious of Adenauer
after the February 1 meeting of the Rhineland Constituent Assembly,
convoked two separatist meetings in Cologne on March 7 and 10,
1919. The separatists withdrew from Adenauer all powers conferred
by the Rhineland committees, vesting them henceforth in the stead-

---

[35] Hans Adam Dorten Papers, The Hoover Institution on War, Revolution
and Peace, Palo Alto, California, Volume II.

fast Dorten. At the Cologne meetings the separatists reaffirmed their objectives: the creation of a Rhenish state to include the entire Rhineland—a state which could alleviate reparations for all of Germany by being a means of reconciliation between France and Germany. The Rhenish people would decide by plebiscite the form of the constitution of the new state.[36]

Dorten and Kastert decided to hold a "pre-plebiscite" by mailing Rhineland independence ballots to the electors of Aachen and Coblenz. According to Dorten, "90 per cent of the cards returned had signatures in our favor; within eight days 52,000 were sent from Aachen, and 42,000 from Coblenz."[37] This was the stuff of which dreams were made. Dorten and Kastert had other cards printed for the "polling" of Cologne, but the British intervened, accusing Kastert of trying to prepare a plebiscite without authorization from the British army. Dorten charged that Adenauer, upon seeing the British opposition, "accepted from the government of Berlin the mission of informing Brockdorff-Rantzau, Germany's chief representative at Versailles, of the situation created by our efforts and furnishing him with arguments to oppose us, if we succeeded in being heard by the Peace Conference."[38] Adenauer later replied to these charges in the following words: "When Dorten proclaimed the Rhine Republic, the political adviser of the British Supreme Commander [Colonel Ryan], upon my advice, prohibited any change of political status within the British zone without permission from the British authorities. I considered this the best means to prevent the spread of the movement Dorten had started to the British zone, especially to Cologne. Dorten's claim that I accepted orders from the Berlin Government to inform Herr Brockdorff-Rantzau about the situation, and to supply him with rebuttals in case Dorten obtained a hearing at the Peace Conference, is pure fiction."[39]

[36] *Die Gruende,* pp. 39–40; cf. Dorten, "Le général Mangin en Rhénanie," p. 41.

[37] Dorten, "Le général Mangin en Rhénanie," p. 41. Dorten later deposited the cards in the Hoover Institution; cf. *Die Gruende,* p. 41.

[38] Dorten, "Le général Mangin en Rhénanie," p. 41.

[39] Letter from Konrad Adenauer to me, 5 September 1956.

Convinced that the mayor of Cologne had become an outright enemy, Kastert transferred the center of his propaganda efforts from Cologne to Aachen, the headquarters of the Belgian zone of occupation.[40] Dorten concentrated his efforts in the South, obtaining in April 1919 the long sought permission to see General Mangin at his headquarters at Mainz. Mangin dazzled him with the "keen intelligence which scintillated from his penetrating glance, a little ironical but compassionate." [41] This is another way of stating that at last Dorten had found a French official who would listen sympathetically. Dorten fondly recalled the occasion: "My first conference lasted an entire morning. Mangin did not let me go before learning everything which had happened, good or bad; I sketched for him at once the character of each of the actors. After that I saw him almost daily to keep him informed, and to explain to him the Rhenish point of view." [42] Clemenceau contended that Mangin never reported these conversations to him.[43]

General Mangin told Dorten that he opposed annexation of the West bank of the Rhine, since that would make it difficult to obtain the vitally needed protective glacis on the East bank. Mangin favored the creation of an independent Rhineland republic, including an adequate zone on the Right bank. He rejected the idea of making such a Rhenish state a part of the Reich, but he was willing to consider at some future date the creation of a Confederation of the Rhine, on the Napoleonic model. The immediate objective was "pure and simple independence." [44]

Dorten had some difficulty in trying to convince General Mangin that the Rhenish people would not accept the cutting of all ties with Germany, much as they might desire an end of Prussian hegemony. He prepared a memorandum for the general, setting forth the desiderata of the Rhineland committees as revised at their last meeting on March 10. The note conceded that the separatists had

---

[40] Dorten, "Le général Mangin en Rhénanie," p. 42.

[41] Dorten, *La tragédie rhénane*, p. 62.

[42] Dorten, *La tragédie rhénane;* see also *Die Gruende*, p. 41.

[43] Clemenceau, *Grandeur and Misery*, p. 214.

[44] Dorten, "Le général Mangin en Rhénanie," p. 45.

been ill-advised to have forced the Rhineland question before being given advance assurance of French support. A new Rhineland state, even if incorporated within the Reich, could enter into direct relations with France. A barrier would be erected against Bolshevism, and a bridge of civilization constructed between West and East. Collaboration between the occupation authorities and the Rhineland government would reduce economic and political difficulties and lessen military burdens. But to achieve these goals it was necessary that France try to prevent the activities of "malevolent persons" in the British and American zones who, with impunity, were spreading hostile propaganda against the Rhineland separatist movement. General Mangin was told that it was essential to end the convenient but shortsighted practice of using the Prussian authorities as intermediaries between the French and the Rhinelanders. The general assured Dorten that he personally would inform his officers of the Rhineland program, and he would propagandize its objectives wherever possible.[45] Dorten had won an enthusiastic convert and one most strategically situated. The separatists went about their propaganda activities with renewed hope, now that they knew that no less than Mangin shared their general objectives.

[45] Dorten, "Le général Mangin en Rhénanie," pp. 47–48.

Chapter III

Foch As Peacemaker

The more the proponents of separatism tried to detach the Rhineland, the greater became British and American opposition. On February 25, 1919, Clemenceau addressed a memoir to Britain and the United States in which he summarized the French position as follows:

The French Government asks the Allied and Associated Powers to insert in the clauses of the preliminaries of the peace the three following principles:

(1) The Western frontier of Germany ought to be fixed at the Rhine;

(2) The Rhine bridges should be occupied by an interallied force;

(3) The above measures should not redound to the advantage of any power in the form of annexation of territory.

These demands were answered on March 11–12, 1919, at a Paris meeting of the *ad hoc* committee of Britain, France, and the United States for the purpose of drawing up the new German boundary. The British representative, Philip Kerr, directed against his French counterpart, André Tardieu, a closely reasoned set of objections to a detached Rhineland. Kerr doubted whether the Rhinelanders could be separated from Germany without their being consulted, or without the betrayal of the very principles of self-determination for which the Allies had fought. As for the claims of a French tradition in the Rhineland, these were the palest of phantoms for much time had passed since 1814 when the French were last stationed in Cologne. Besides, the historical argument had been worn too threadbare by Germany in rationalizing its recent possession of Alsace-Lorraine for it to have much cogency when applied by France. Kerr declared to Tardieu and to the American representative, Sidney Mezes, that Britain was opposed to a permanent army of occupation on the Rhine, and to the stationing of British troops for any considerable length of time outside British territory. An occupation army would be certain to create nationalistic irritation not only on the Left bank of the Rhine but throughout all of Germany. Britain regarded an independent state on the West bank as a source of weakness and an unnecessary complication. What would the Allies do in the event a "sovereign" Rhineland state at a later date tolerated agitation for a reunion with Germany? Would the Allied occupation troops be used to suppress unionist demonstrations? If local conflicts led to war, the British Empire would have little of that solidarity with France which it displayed from 1914 through 1918.[1]

André Tardieu asserted that his government's objectives were not in the least imperialistic. Moreover, the League of Nations would provide a means for orderly evolution in Franco-German relations. He declared that France, after its immense suffering, should have the choice of methods in preventing a recurrence of German invasion, and if public opinion outside France were hostile to the Rhineland proposal, it could be enlightened. Tardieu denied that the Rhinelanders would revolt, since they were being offered not annexation but independence, security against Bolshevism, and relief from the burden of a war indemnity. The only predictable revolt was "the certain revolt of French opinion against a peace which would not include the occupation of the Rhine."[2]

Clemenceau felt deep concern over Allied intransigence. In private conversation with Lloyd George he repeated that France with its 40,000,000 inhabitants could not be allowed to face in isolation a hostile Germany of 65,000,000 population with a footing on both sides of the Rhine. If England were so opposed, heart and soul, to a detached Rhineland, did it have any counter-proposal to offer France as a substitute for the Rhine barrier? Thus challenged, Lloyd George made a historic decision which he described as follows:

[1] *Annales de la Chambre* . . . Séance du 2 septembre 1919, p. 3679; Tardieu, *The Truth About the Treaty,* pp. 172–173.

[2] Tardieu, pp. 173–175.

I then conceived the idea of a joint military guarantee by America and Britain to France against any aggression by Germany in the future. President Wilson agreed to this proposal. On the 14th of March, 1919, President Wilson and I informed M. Clemenceau that we could not consent to any occupation of the Left bank of the Rhine except a short occupation as provisional guarantee for payment of the German debt. On the other hand, we formally offered our immediate military guarantee against any unprovoked aggression on the part of Germany against France.[3]

In taking cognizance of this offer, Clemenceau, on March 17, addressed to the chiefs of the Allied governments a note in which he reiterated the French Rhineland demands as set forth previously by Marshal Foch, and most recently in the French memoir of February 25, 1919. Clemenceau once again insisted upon the military occupation of the Rhine by an interallied force, to take effect at once and to be permanent. The Left bank was to be severed from the Reich and from the German customs union. By removing from Germany such advantages for an aggressor as possession of the Left bank, its railways and the Rhine bridges, France could be spared a third invasion. Since France had been deprived of the Russian alliance and lacked good natural frontiers, a military occupation could offset these handicaps by making possible the arrival of Allied military assistance for safeguarding the channel ports and the railways. German disarmament would be no more adequate a guarantee in itself than the League of Nations. A physical guarantee was necessary. As for the objections advanced against these claims, Clemenceau contended that there was not likely to be on the Left bank a movement for unification with Germany, since the Left bank was different from the rest of Germany, and besides it dreaded Bolshevism and the prospect of a war indemnity. It was conscious of its own economic interests. It hated Prussian functionaries assigned to it by the Empire. Separatist tendencies had already become manifest there, despite "the absolute reserve" of the French. As for the proffered Anglo-American alliance, France was fully appreciative of its high value, but even this guarantee could not prevent France from having to stand alone against the aggressor until such time as the Allies could arrive

[3] Lloyd George, *The Truth*, 402–403.

on French soil. The proposed alliance was the substitution of a temporal for a spatial guarantee, and to be completely safe France needed both.[4]

After a month of continued negotiations, Clemenceau extracted from Wilson and Lloyd George the agreement that the demilitarized zone on the Right bank would be fifty kilometers in depth and would be permanently disarmed. But Clemenceau had to abandon his insistence upon the permanent military occupation of the Rhine, which Wilson and Lloyd George steadfastly rejected. A schedule of Rhineland occupation was finally accepted by all three statesmen. It provided for an occupation of fifteen years at the Mainz bridgehead, ten years at the Coblenz bridgehead, and five years at Cologne. As insurance for France in case the United States Senate or British Parliament failed to ratify the proposed Anglo-American military guarantee, there was stated in what was to become Article 429 of the treaty: "If, at that date [the end of fifteen years], the guarantees against unprovoked aggression by Germany are not considered sufficient by the Allied and Associated Governments, the evacuation of the occupying troops may be delayed to the extent regarded as necessary for the purpose of obtaining the required guarantees." [5] Of equal importance to France as a potential safeguard for the future was the right of reoccupying the Rhineland even after evacuation, if Germany, in the judgment of the Reparation Commission, did not execute all reparation provisions of the treaty (Article 430).[6]

Clemenceau, in a later discussion of this momentous compromise with his private secretary, Jean Martet, gave the following defense of its provisions:

We are only in the Rhineland to ensure the execution of the Treaty. If the Boches fulfill their contract we leave. If they do not fulfill it we remain . . . a hundred years if necessary, until they have paid whatever they owe us—and we shall do it by virtue of Articles 428, 429, and 430 of the Treaty, whose existence no one seems to suspect. . . . And if, once we have evacuated, the Boches violate their contract . . . we shall reoccupy

[4] Clemenceau's note is quoted in full in Lhopital, *Foch, l'armistice et la paix,* pp. 150–159.

[5] Tardieu, p. 211.

[6] Recouly, *Le mémorial de Foch,* p. 196.

the territory, still by virtue of these articles. Well, we have the Rhine, haven't we? What more does anyone want? That we . . . annex the Rhineland? It would be the same as renouncing all that we fought for. After having won with the help of the English and Americans, it would be equivalent to saying to them at the moment that the job is finished . . . "and now we shall take this, we shall take that. . . ." "I beg your pardon," the English and Americans could properly answer, "you will take, you will take! But what you are going to take doesn't belong to you alone. There are three of us who helped bring the wild beast down." [7]

Clemenceau's compromise agreement in no way satisfied Foch. The marshal, in a conversation with Raymond Recouly, emphasized the fact that the United States Senate had to ratify a military alliance by a two-thirds majority—a very uncertain contingency. Even if ratified by Washington and London, the proffered military alliance would be difficult of execution because of the inevitable delay before British and American troops could come to the rescue of France in the event of a surprise attack from Germany. Foch contended that a provisional occupation of the Rhine, albeit with the right of extension of time, was no solution of the German menace. "It commits us necessarily to a course strewn with difficulties, with differences, with quarrels with the Germans as well as with our Allies. Who will judge the failure to carry out the treaty? We alone? Or with our Allies? How can we expect this agreement to last indefinitely? This hope is contrary to good sense." [8]

Foch's misgivings with regard to the ratification of the proposed military alliance by the United States Senate were, of course, well founded. Within a year of Clemenceau's acceptance of the offer it was to be sidetracked by the Senate, and as a consequence it was also to lapse as far as the British government was concerned. Did this repudiation by France's Allies demonstrate the bankruptcy of Clemenceau's German policy? Foch thought so, but was the marshal justified in his strictures? Despite the seeming confirmation of Foch's jeremiads by the German invasion of 1940, Clemenceau pursued the

---

[7] Jean Martet, *Georges Clemenceau* (London, 1930), pp. 150–151; cf. Major Louis Eugène Mangin, *La France et le Rhin* (Genève, 1945), pp. 31–33; see also Grimm, *Poincaré am Rhein,* pp. 18–20.

[8] Recouly, pp. 194–197.

only course possible in the straitened circumstances of 1919. Had France ignored the objections of its wartime Allies and acted unilaterally in the Rhineland, either by annexing the region or by contriving a buffer state there, the inevitable German retaliation would have found the French completely isolated, with London and Washington in all probability tendering at least moral support to Berlin against "French imperialism." Clemenceau's compromise prevented this worst of all catastrophes. Moreover, Article 430 of the Treaty of Versailles permitted France to return to the Rhineland to block its remilitarization by Germany. That France did not call Hitler's bluff in 1935 or 1936 was not the fault of Clemenceau, for he provided his country with all the legal weapons needed for the punishment of Germany in event of the violation of the Treaty. A French return to the Rhineland in 1936 to expel Hitler's Wehrmacht would not only have been sanctioned by the Peace Treaty, but it would have won the uneasy acquiescence, if not the active support, of London and Washington. Herein lay Clemenceau's vindication. He forged the indispensable politico-military weapon. A feckless government chose not to use it at the time of crisis. Foch looked only for a simple military solution—the physical occupation of the Rhine—and he ignored the intricate political factors involved.

Foch complained to Recouly that Clemenceau kept him in the dark during the Paris Conference with regard to the Rhineland negotiations. "I was informed of what happened only very imperfectly. One could say without exaggeration that the government and the principals concerned took care not to inform me at all." Foch's demands for drawing the military frontier of Germany at the Rhine, for stationing an Allied army at the river until Germany had met all the stipulations of the treaty, and for forming an intermediate Rhineland state between France and Germany, were, he pointed out, all apparently disregarded by the French government. "Now the question of security primarily concerned me, and on this point I was resolved to make myself heard not only by the French government, but by the Allied governments. . . . I decided to do everything humanly within my power and even beyond to oppose this disastrous solution." [9]

[9] Recouly, p. 199.

To carry out this resolution, Foch sent a letter to Clemenceau on March 30, urgently requesting that he be allowed to address the Council of Paris on the grave necessity of drawing the military frontier of Western Europe at the Rhine. Clemenceau readily agreed, arranging a meeting of the Big Four the following day. Foch read a memorandum in which he repeated all of his now familiar arguments for the Rhine barrier. He declared that a neutral or demilitarized zone along the Rhine (such as Lloyd George and Wilson had accepted) would not be a sufficient guarantee, since the Germans could cross it by a surprise attack, confronting France with a *fait accompli*. It would then be necessary for the French and Belgians to attempt to rally on their eastern frontiers, unprotected by natural obstacles, to await the eventual arrival of the British and American Allies—a matter of weeks for the British who would have to cross the Channel, and months for the remote Americans. This would risk a repetition of the 1914 disaster. Consequently, it was vitally necessary for the Allies to remain entrenched along the watercourse of the Rhine.[10] Lloyd George noted in his account of the meeting that Foch received no support for his cherished plan from any of the Allied commanders-in-chief who were present, nor was he to be supported by King Albert of Belgium who expressed his disapproval several days later.[11] As for President Wilson, he was already bored with Foch's reiteration of France's case on the Rhineland. "Foch may be a great general," Wilson remarked to Ray Stannard Baker, "but he is a dull man."[12]

The marshal seemed to consider perverse any viewpoint or statement of Clemenceau's which did not coincide with his own recommendations. Foch now complained that while Clemenceau, "authoritarian, domineering, and blunt," was compelled to listen to advocacy of the Rhineland scheme for form's sake on two or three occasions, "he was resolved to take no account of it."[13] With equal

---

[10] Mantoux, ed., *Les délibérations du conseil des quatre*, I, 92–94; cf. Terrail, *Le combat des trois*, p. 220.

[11] Lloyd George, *The Truth*, I, 424; cf. Mordacq, *Le ministère Clemenceau*, III, 210.

[12] Ray Stannard Baker Papers, 1919, Library of Congress, Washington, D.C.

[13] Recouly, *Le mémorial de Foch*, p. 203.

justice one could say that the marshal was resolved to take no account of the inflexible Allied opposition to a truncated Germany. Nor did he seem to be aware of the plight in which France would find itself if it alienated its allies.

Foch knew how to display a mulish obstinacy. Isaiah Bowman, the Chief Territorial Adviser of the American Peace Commission, related that following a session of the Supreme War Council at which the Western boundary of Poland was discussed, Foch refused to leave the room to allow the civilian heads of state to deliberate in the absence of the military representatives as was their custom. Clemenceau repeated pointedly: "Now that the business of the Supreme War Council has ended, the military men and naval experts will please retire." Foch twice ignored the cue, refusing to budge. Clemenceau, at a loss, rose from his chair and went over to President Wilson with the comment: "I don't know what to do; he won't leave." It was generally understood that the military were to attend only if there was something in dispute which required their presence. Arthur Balfour, British Foreign Secretary, tactfully attempted a *détente* by remarking: "I suggest we have tea." Foch, self-invited, stayed on for tea. Bowman reported that Clemenceau grew increasingly exasperated and apparently concluded that, since hints were lost upon the marshal, the frontal approach was the only course remaining. Clemenceau walked over to Foch and said something in a low voice which produced the desired result of the marshal's departure.[14]

Determined to renew his campaign against a merely temporary occupation of the Rhineland, Foch wrote Clemenceau again on April 6, a week after addressing the Big Four: "As pourparlers between the heads of the Allied governments get under way, commitments could be made which might be difficult to abandon. It seems indispensable for me to meet with the French delegation to learn the exact state of negotiations." [15] Three days later Clemenceau replied ("disagreeably enough," in Foch's opinion) to the effect that as Allied generalissimo Foch had the right to speak and to make

[14] House and Seymour, eds., *What Really Happened at Paris*, pp. 462–463.
[15] Recouly, p. 205.

his opinion known, but not to deliberate with the members of the French peace delegation. It was the government alone which deliberated, but it would be glad to hear him on all questions of a military nature. Clemenceau promised that he would soon invite the marshal to "set forth his views before the Council of Ministers, in the presence of the French delegation." [16]

A week passed and nothing happened. Foch, growing restive, addressed still another letter to Clemenceau on April 15, asking once again to be heard by the Council of Ministers and the French delegation. He expressed his formal disapproval of the compromise being prepared: "The occupation of the Rhineland for a period of fifteen years, with successive withdrawals, [appears] from the military standpoint unacceptable for France. It would leave us in complete insecurity, both as to the defense of territory and the payment of indemnities. It [is] necessary to hold the line of the Rhine which, moreover, would require far less effectives than any other method."

Not content with his own importunities, Foch wrote Poincaré to enlist the services of the President of the Republic in arranging a meeting of the Council of Ministers to hear his views. Poincaré duly forwarded Foch's letter to Clemenceau. The Tiger replied that he would summon the marshal "as soon as he was ready, and he added that nothing definite would be done [on the Rhineland question] beforehand." Foch was highly skeptical of this reassurance. As he expressed it: "It was at this time that M. Clemenceau discussed with President Wilson and Lloyd George the policy of our temporary occupation of the Rhineland. He had already accepted the principle sometime previously. . . . It is difficult to pretend that the acceptance of this principle did not constitute an important commitment on the part of the French government." [17]

Heightening Marshal Foch's suspicion that Clemenceau would confront him with an accomplished fact in diplomacy was a telegram which the marshal received from the President of the Council on April 17. The marshal was ordered to make travel arrangements through General Nudant, the French representative on the Armistice

[16] Recouly, p. 205.
[17] Recouly, pp. 207–208.

Commission at Spa, for the German delegates who were to go to Versailles on April 25 to receive the preliminary text of the forthcoming peace treaty. "The German Government," Clemenceau telegraphed, "should . . . be requested through General Nudant to indicate as soon as possible the names and [status] of the delegates it proposes to send to Versailles, also the number, names and [status] of the persons in their suite. It will be for you, Monsieur le maréchal, to be so good as to give all proper instructions for the conveyance and arrival of the German delegation." [18]

Clemenceau's simple command infuriated Foch to the point of outright insubordination. In a letter to Clemenceau he flatly refused to transmit the travel orders to Spa on the pretext that his instructions were not precise, since he was not told at the outset either the number or status of the German delegates. The real reason for his disobedience was that, despite the promised hearing by the Council of Ministers before definite diplomatic commitments were made, Clemenceau's summoning of the German delegation was the strongest indication that the French government, for all practical purposes, had already yielded to the British and American views on the acceptability of a temporary, fifteen-year occupation of the Rhine. "For these different reasons," the marshal explained, "I refused to send the telegram in my name to General Nudant. If M. Clemenceau, I said, insists upon this telegram, he has only to send it . . . himself as Minister of War." [19]

The day following Foch's open defiance of civilian authority, Clemenceau had a conference with him and bitterly reproached him for insubordination. The marshal stood his ground, replying, "I will always act thus. I will never give to my subordinates an order which I myself do not understand." Clemenceau became enraged over this patent quibbling and told the marshal: "Things cannot go on this way." Foch coolly retorted: "You may do whatever you like." [20]

When Clemenceau discussed this incident with his military adviser, the conciliatory and tactful General Mordacq, the President

[18] Clemenceau, *Grandeur and Misery*, pp. 131–132.
[19] Recouly, *Le mémorial de Foch*, pp. 229–230.
[20] Recouly, p. 231; cf. Bugnet, *Foch Speaks*, pp. 272–273.

of the Council observed that "the first duty of a soldier was to obey, and if the marshal, so inured to discipline, took this attitude, it was because of some ulterior motive, because . . . he was trying to bring off some coup." [21]

Clemenceau was prepared to dismiss Foch for flouting an order from his government, and he sent General Mordacq to see the more pliant Marshal Pétain at Chantilly to discuss with him the prospect of succeeding Foch. Determined to play the role of peacemaker, General Mordacq explained the rift to Marshal Pétain as being due to "some misunderstanding." Pétain, who knew how to be the soul of correctness when he wished, readily agreed.

But Clemenceau was not to be immediately pacified. When he showed Foch's letter of defiance to Wilson and Lloyd George, the American President was moved to remark: "I will not entrust the American Army to a general who does not obey his government." [22] Clemenceau was stung anew by this taunt. The Tiger, accompanied by Foreign Minister Pichon, went to the Elysée Palace to give an account of the insubordination to President Poincaré, who was known to be Foch's supporter on the Rhineland question. He wanted to explain in advance his forthcoming dismissal of the marshal, which would be certain to produce resounding political repercussions in Parliament as well as throughout the nation.

Upon Clemenceau's return to his office at Rue St. Dominique, his military adviser tried to mediate the dispute. "A man like you," General Mordacq told him, "ought not to condemn a person without a hearing. I would guarantee that a conversation between you and the marshal, man to man, without anyone else present, would clear up matters in a few minutes. Let me go and find the marshal to-morrow morning. I will bring him here and before 11 o'clock the incident will be closed." [23] Clemenceau agreed, and meanwhile sent the telegram in question to General Nudant—"taking care," as he explained, "to refer in it to the Commander-in-Chief's refusal, so that there might remain a material record of the delinquency." [24]

---

[21] Mordacq, *Le ministère Clemenceau*, III, 227.
[22] Clemenceau, *Grandeur and Misery*, p. 132; cf. Mordacq, III, 228.
[23] Mordacq, III, 229.
[24] Clemenceau, p. 134; cf. Tardieu, *The Truth About the Treaty*, p. 188.

The conference with the marshal was more amicable than might have been expected. Foch rationalized his letter as an infelicitously worded request for more information on the travel arrangements for the German delegation. He conceded that the wording might have been "open to question," but not understanding very well the orders which he was asked to send, he wanted to spare General Nudant at Spa the same confusion and embarrassment.[25] Clemenceau accepted this far-fetched excuse to put an end to the dispute, but he recorded his opinion of Foch's underlying motives:

As the general [sic] had no reason, or no seeming reason, to refuse to dispatch the telegram I sent him, I am obliged to believe that he simply desired to delay the arrival of the plenipotentiaries in order to give himself time to develop once more his obsessive thesis of French cannon upon the Rhine. . . . So he blocked the path of the Allied Powers. . . . What would he have said if I had refused him my support because I found fault with one of his military operations? . . . After a lapse of a few days, intended to give an opportunity for repenting, I was authorized by the Allies to continue Foch in his post if he promised on his honor not to behave in the same way again. He pledged himself to everything I asked of him.[26]

Clemenceau's interpretation is plausible, but it must be recalled that he had given Foch two explicit promises (in response to his letters of April 6 and 15) that the marshal would be allowed to address the Council of Ministers and the French delegation before anything "definite would be done" on the Rhineland question. Yet the very act of summoning the German delegation to Versailles for April 25 would make an empty gesture of any appearance of Foch before the French Cabinet and delegation, since the Rhine policy appeared all but set for a limited occupation. Foch regarded this as calculated duplicity on Clemenceau's part. The incident put not only Foch but also the Tiger in an unfavorable light. Clemenceau had good and sufficient reasons for accepting Lloyd George's compromise formula for the Rhineland. But he might very well have summoned Marshal Foch and explained to him the entire diplomatic situation, elaborating the reasons why France could not afford to

[25] Mordacq, III, 230–231; cf. Tardieu, p. 188.
[26] Clemenceau, p. 134.

alienate Britain and America. Probably Foch would not have been convinced by any such line of reasoning, but it would have relieved Clemenceau of the charge of duplicity. Clemenceau evidently wanted to avoid the political furor in France which a premature disclosure of the abandonment of a permanently detached Rhineland would be likely to create, thereby jeopardizing the treaty's acceptance. Even the doughtiest of fighters does not relish constant combat, and Clemenceau had taken the devious way out of the French domestic implications of the Rhineland problem. Clemenceau's error was psychological and in the realm of tact, courtesy, and harmonious personal relations; Foch's dereliction was legal and patent—and he was caught red-handed, and quite properly taken to task.

Heedless of his narrow escape from dismissal, Marshal Foch charged immediately from one questionable venture into another. The marshal was either presuming upon his indispensability because of the vast prestige and adulation which he enjoyed, or else he was so devoted to his soldierly conception of France's strategic interests that he was willing to incur personal risk to block a temporary occupation of the Rhine. He said at the time of the insubordination incident that "there was only a very feeble chance of putting an obstacle in the way of a solution which seemed . . . to be disastrous, but which was being undertaken, but that chance was worth the effort." [27] To exploit that "feeble chance" the marshal now had recourse to the press, arranging for the publication of two highly controversial newspaper articles on the Rhineland question, both of which appeared on April 19, 1919.

The first article was anonymous, but according to André Tardieu it was "inspired by [Foch] and its proofs had been corrected by one of his officers." [28] To circumvent the censor, *Le Matin* published it under the vague heading, "The Military Doctrine of the Defense of the Rhine." An unnamed French officer was quoted as advancing the familiar argument that the Left bank of the Rhine should be retained until Germany had paid off "the last centime" of its reparations debt,

[27] Recouly, *Le mémorial de Foch,* pp. 207–208.
[28] Tardieu, p. 187; cf. Mantoux, ed., *Les délibérations du conseil des quatre,* **II,** 443–444.

and "until the political situation of Europe and Germany permits us to evacuate without any risk." The Rhine was Western Europe's only good military frontier, shorter and easier to defend than the eastern frontiers of France, Luxembourg, and Belgium. Ten to fifteen divisions of Allied troops—French, Belgian, and British—would suffice to hold it. In event of renewed German aggression, the Allied occupation force would either use the Rhine as a "fulcrum of resistance," or it could withdraw after blowing up all bridges, railways, and installations—no small advantage for a France fatally destined to wait for weeks before the arrival of aid from its Allies. The Rhine as a military frontier would safeguard all the Western world, not merely France. As for the argument that a detached Rhineland would violate its inhabitants' rights of self-determination, the article in *Le Matin* contended that "military frontiers and political frontiers have nothing in common. The inhabitants will govern themselves in their own fashion, and will never be induced, directly or indirectly, by any form of pressure, to break the bonds which unite them with Germany." [29]

The second article appeared in the London edition of *The Daily Mail,* the Paris edition of the paper having to omit it because of the French censor's disapproval of its attribution to Foch. For this was a credited interview which Marshal Foch gave to the British journalist G. Ward Price.

Having reached the Rhine [Foch told Price], we must stay there. Impress that upon your fellow countrymen. . . . We must have a barrier. . . . Democracies like ours, which are never aggressive, must have strong natural frontiers. Remember, that these seventy millions of Germans will always be a menace to us. . . . They are a people both envious and warlike. . . . Fifty years hence they will be what they are today. What was it that saved the Allies at the beginning of the war? Russia. Well, on whose side will Russia be in the future? With us or with the Germans . . . ? The Allied armies? Where will the Allied armies be? The British army will be in Canada, in Australia, in New Zealand. The American army will be in the United States. . . . And next time, remember, the Germans will make no mistake. They will break through into

[29] *Le Matin,* April 19, 1919.

Northern France and will seize the Channel ports as a base of operations against England. . . .[30]

This remarkably prophetic interview brought immediate repercussions from President Wilson and Prime Minister Lloyd George, who strongly protested to Clemenceau:

We very willingly placed our armies under the supreme command of a French general for whom we have the highest admiration and the deepest gratitude. But this general, no matter how great his glory, is an obstacle to the decisions of the Governments. We cannot accept this situation and permit the authority we have conferred to be turned against us. It is a fundamental question of constitutional responsibility. We are, today as yesterday, ready to accept a French general as Commander-in-Chief. But we must have a general who obeys the Governments.[31]

Clemenceau promised to see Foch about his latest intervention. The Tiger confided to André Tardieu that he hoped that a storm would be averted. "Although [Foch] has unquestionably put himself in the wrong," he said, "I want to get him out of it. I don't want the Chief of Victory to be touched." [32]

When Clemenceau asked Foch for an explanation of his latest excursion into the political realm, the marshal replied disingenuously that he knew "nothing of the newspaper articles." [33] As for the officer who was alleged to have read the proofs, Marshal Foch said that he "was at that moment on the way to Angoulême." In Clemenceau's judgment, this was "an evasive statement. It is easy to take a train after correcting a set of proofs." [34]

Foch, in his later version, seemed to have forgotten about this denial, for he acknowledged: "I simply gave an interview to *The Daily Mail* to say what I thought of the treaty which was being drawn up. The publication of this interview was forbidden by the censor. Clemenceau, the domineering Jacobin, was reluctant to yield

---

[30] *The Daily Mail*, April 19, 1919.

[31] Tardieu, *The Truth About the Treaty*, p. 188; cf. Clemenceau, *Grandeur and Misery*, p. 125.

[32] Tardieu, p. 188.

[33] Tardieu, p. 188; cf. Mantoux, *Les délibérations*, II, 443–444.

[34] Clemenceau, p. 125 n.

to the idea that someone else, especially a military man, was intervening in the negotiations which he was conducting and which he intended to conduct alone." [35]

Tardieu gave an account of the incident of the newspaper articles which was friendly to both parties. According to him, when Clemenceau accusingly named the officer who corrected the proofs of the article, the marshal remained silent. Clemenceau said: "Come, you are sorry for all that, aren't you?" The marshal answered, "I regret it with all my heart." Clemenceau, full of cordiality, asked him not to allow himself to be used by journalists and politicians. Clemenceau telephoned the result of his interview to President Poincaré, and the next morning, April 20, at ten o'clock, he informed Lloyd George and Wilson that the matter was settled, that there had been a misunderstanding, and that Marshal Foch was sorry. The two heads of government let the matter drop.[36]

Tardieu's genial version is probably correct in substance, since as a Peace Conference delegate he was advantageously placed between the French civil and military heads. With the advantage of hindsight, one must concede the prescience of Marshal Foch in his gloomy forebodings, even as to many details in *The Daily Mail* interview: the resurgence of German bellicosity by 1939; Russia's siding with Germany, in effect, through the Molotov-Ribbentrop pact; the dispersal of the British armies; the remoteness of the minuscule army of neutral America; and finally, in 1940, the dreaded German break-through into Northern France and the seizure of the Channel ports. Did this clear insight into future possibilities justify Foch in campaigning in the press against the forthcoming Treaty of Versailles? Legally and technically speaking, Foch was clearly outside his strategic province in trying to dictate the political outlines of the treaty. His premonition in regard to a Rhineland only temporarily occupied (which an indecisive French government in 1936 declined to reoccupy) was well founded, as the catastrophe of 1940 was to prove. But the variables and contingencies of the Rhineland question were perceptively outlined by Peace Conference delegate

[35] Recouly, *Le mémorial de Foch,* pp. 231–232.
[36] Tardieu, p. 189.

Jules Cambon, toward the end of his life, when he wrote: "I have had the feeling that if we had persisted in our desire to have the Left bank of the Rhine, there would have been a new war and without England and the United States on our side, for they were always opposed to our claims on this subject."[37] Because of Clemenceau's reluctant acquiescence in British and American opposition to a truncated Germany, France had at least a British ally during its mortal peril in 1940, as well as a guilt-ridden American well-wisher, both of whom rescued it four years later. France's prospects of ultimate salvation would have been illusory indeed if Foch's well-intentioned persistence had actually resulted in French unilateral amputation of a Germany which remained otherwise unoccupied, only partially disarmed, and implacably bent upon revenge. Moreover, physical control of a disaffected Rhenish puppet state would hardly have added to France's stature, and the desire of such a puppet to rejoin Germany would have been as predictable as the reunion of the Saar to Germany.

Marshal Foch had by no means exhausted his arsenal of weapons in his campaign against Clemenceau's Rhineland compromise. Unutilized as yet was the threat of resignation which the marshal's close ally, President Poincaré, could be called upon to employ before Foch had to resort to it himself. The marshal asserted in his memoirs "that the President of the Republic himself, M. Poincaré, was entirely in agreement with me on this question of security. He also had the conviction that the treaty being prepared would sacrifice the essential interests of France, would deprive our country of the one good frontier which it had the right and duty to demand."[38] Poincaré had been one of the earliest advocates of a detached Rhineland. Foch and Poincaré, insufficiently informed of Clemenceau's protracted diplomatic struggle with Wilson and Lloyd George, entertained the fond hope that the French government could successfully put before the Allies, at the last moment and as an ultimatum, their conception of a permanently detached Rhineland.[39]

[37] Jules Cambon, "La paix: notes inédites, 1919," *La Revue de Paris* (November 1, 1937), pp. 30–31.

[38] Recouly, p. 209.

[39] Terrail, *Le combat des trois*, p. 225.

Clemenceau heard a rumor to the effect that President Poincaré had been holding "conferences" on the Rhineland question with the Presidents of the two Chambers and with Marshal Foch. The Tiger conceded that

. . . it was indisputably his right, but in my opinion he should have notified his Prime Minister. . . . From the constitutional point of view these "conferences" between the President of the Republic and Marshal Foch, my subordinate, should obviously not have taken place unknown to me. . . . The question of the Rhine implied such changes in our future policy with regard to the peace that neither Marshal Foch nor the Presidents of the Chambers were in a position to decide it.[40]

It was bruited about that in addition to Foch and Poincaré, Peace Conference Delegate Jules Cambon and even some members of Clemenceau's Cabinet were adamant in their demands for a permanently detached Rhineland. Poincaré wrote Clemenceau to request an opportunity for Foch to address the Council of Ministers and the Peace Delegation to express once again his opposition to a compromise on Rhineland security. Clemenceau had heard that Poincaré at the last minute would deliver an ultimatum to the Government in which he would assert that, if Marshal Foch's proposals were not accepted, the President of the Republic would resign.[41] Clemenceau told his military adviser, General Mordacq, that he expected "a hard battle" on April 25, the day he had set for the session.[42]

The long expected showdown between Clemenceau, Foch, and Poincaré appeared to be at hand. Attending the tense session, in addition to the Council of Ministers and Poincaré, were Marshal Foch, his Chief of Staff General Maxime Weygand, André Tardieu, and Jules Cambon. When the "guests" had been introduced, Foch received the Tiger's permission to distribute copies of his Rhineland memoranda of January 10 and March 31. The marshal requested that minutes of the session be taken, which Clemenceau refused to allow, although he said that General Weygand could take informal notes which would not have legal validity. Bearing in mind the

[40] Martet, *Georges Clemenceau*, p. 148.
[41] Terrail, p. 226.
[42] Mordacq, *Le ministère Clemenceau*, III, 264.

rumor of Poincaré's impending coup, Clemenceau said to Foch: "You will be able to express all of your ideas . . . everything. Following that, the government will deliberate." The Tiger added for Poincaré's benefit: "The Council of Ministers will deliberate alone. I will withdraw if a discussion should begin in which persons take part who have no right under the constitution to deliberate with the government, and who are here only in a consultative capacity."[43]

Foch told the group that he could not discuss the draft of the treaty being prepared, since he was denied knowledge of it. However, he wanted to set forth the military conditions which he believed should be incorporated in the treaty. Foch abstracted the essential parts of his memoranda of January 10 and March 31, his thesis being the same as always: the Rhine as France's military frontier, and its occupation until the Germans carried out fully all the conditions of the treaty of peace. No one interrupted him. After he finished speaking, Minister of Armament and Aviation Louis Loucheur asked if he proposed a perpetual occupation of the Rhine. Foch replied that the occupation should last until Germany had paid all the reparations owed.[44]

Silence ensued as Foch's supporters waited for Pioncaré's expected intervention. But Poincaré astonished Clemenceau by remaining as mute as the others. The Tiger thereupon dismissed Jules Cambon and André Tardieu as well as the marshal and his chief of staff. When the "guests" reached the antechamber, Cambon, having noticed that the marshal had carefully gathered up his notes before withdrawing, said to him: "Ah, Marshal, you collect your little papers!" Foch retorted in a fury: "I keep them, Mister Ambassador, as you would do well with yours."[45] After allowing this cryptic remark to be absorbed, Foch added: "We shall all be accused of treason because the nation will never understand that from our victory bankruptcy is likely to come."[46]

[43] Terrail, *Le combat des trois,* pp. 226–227; cf. Lhopital, *Foch l'armistice et la paix,* pp. 201–202.

[44] Lhopital, p. 207.

[45] Alain Mellet, "Foch et la paix," *La Revue Universelle* (April 15, 1929), pp. 986–987.

[46] Bugnet, *Foch Speaks,* pp. 271–272.

This was too much for André Tardieu, Clemenceau's staunch supporter in the protracted peace negotiations. Having reached the door, he turned upon Foch and said: "You speak like a factious general!" [47] Tardieu added the comment that with an occupation of fifteen years, extensible beyond that time if necessary, and with France's promised alliances, the nation's security was complete. This observation provoked Jules Cambon to exclaim: "Alliances! You believe in them! I do so less than you. If I had been questioned I would have said so, but no one asked me." [48] Tardieu optimistically reminded them of the reinsurance provision of the treaty whereunder the Rhineland could be occupied beyond the fifteen-year period if the guarantees against unprovoked aggression by Germany were not considered sufficient by the Allied and Associated Governments.[49]

While the spirited exchange between Foch, Tardieu, and Cambon was taking place in the antechamber, the Council of Ministers deliberated upon the treaty draft. Prime Minister Clemenceau gave his Cabinet a detailed account of his long diplomatic battle over the Rhineland. He reported that the entire French Peace Delegation, not merely Marshal Foch, had wanted a permanently detached Rhineland, but Britain and the United States were adamantly opposed. When they offered a tripartite military guarantee to France, was it possible "to reply to them that we had no confidence in their commitment?" [50] By yielding to Allied wishes France could assure a Rhineland occupation which, in event of necessity, would have the support of two powerful allies.

Clemenceau concluded the defense of the proposed treaty by calling attention to the effect of technological changes upon "strategic frontiers." "When one considers the changes brought about in armament, would not the advantage presented by a permanent occupation appear diminished? When one waged war only on foot and with short range artillery, holding the enemy far from the frontier was

[47] Mellet, p. 187.
[48] Terrail, *Le combat des trois*, p. 228; cf. Recouly, *Le mémorial de Foch*, pp. 221–222; see also Lhopital, *Foch, l'armistice et la paix*, pp. 214–215.
[49] Tardieu, *The Truth About the Treaty*, p. 212.
[50] Terrail, p. 230.

very reassuring. But with planes, and with guns firing 150 kilometres, was not the fundamental idea of warfare revolutionized? Would our presence on the Rhine prevent German planes from coming to destroy our cities, if Germany could rebuild an air force?" [51] Those who held that it was still of value to use the Rhine as a glacis between France and Germany could be satisfied nonetheless, "since according to the treaty, we [could] remain alone on the Rhine, and finally, would we not remain there until the Germans had fulfilled all the conditions imposed? Was this not, at bottom, what the Commander-in-Chief of the Allied armies had demanded?" [52]

Clemenceau's speech was followed by Foreign Minister Pichon's account of the principal provisions of the treaty. President of the Republic Poincaré refused to enter the discussion of the treaty, merely summarizing Marshal Foch's proposals and listing the decisions reached by Clemenceau. There remained only the voting on the treaty, and the Cabinet's approval was unanimous. Jules Cambon was instructed to submit the draft to the German plenipotentiary, Count Brockdorff-Rantzau, on May 7. [53]

President Poincaré's "coup" did not come off. Had he threatened to resign unless Foch's Rhineland scheme were insisted upon by the French government, the Council of Ministers would have been in a quandary. Clemenceau might have been formally charged with reopening the entire Rhineland question with the Allies. But would Clemenceau not have resigned rather than accept a seriously intended mandate for that hopeless task? Poincaré, as a responsible and perceptive politician, certainly realized that the resignation of the "Father of Victory" would have been as seismic a political occurrence as Foch's resignation. The President of the Republic would hardly have dared assume the responsibility for touching off such a political disturbance in the midst of the delicate peace negotiations which the Tiger had just detailed for the Cabinet's instruction. Poincaré's "patriotic" abstention spared France a grave governmental crisis before the peace treaty could be signed.

[51] Terrail, p. 230.
[52] Mordacq, *Le ministère Clemenceau*, III, 245.
[53] Terrail, pp. 230–231.

Clemenceau was a complex and contradictory personality. After easily winning his bout with Poincaré over the acceptance of the treaty draft, he seemingly swung around and on April 28, only three days after his victory, he told Poincaré that it might be "useful to make a new effort" to win Britain and America over to a prolongation of the Rhineland occupation! Clemenceau was thoroughly disingenuous in making this bland suggestion, for he was merely trying to placate Poincaré and Foch. But Poincaré responded with alacrity, and proposed to write Clemenceau a letter to be forwarded to Wilson and Lloyd George. In it Poincaré would try to point out the necessity of a territorial pledge until the complete payment of the German debt. Clemenceau agreed, and Poincaré addressed him a long letter of the same date, April 28, 1919.

The President of the Republic began with the suggestion to the Prime Minister that he might submit his views on the Rhineland question to the Allied governments. Poincaré wrote that the war indemnity which the Allies were going to levy upon Germany had not yet been totaled by the Reparation Commission, but it was already apparent that reparation payments would be made over a period of at least thirty years. "It would be just and logical for the military occupation of the Left bank of the Rhine and the bridge-heads to last for the same period." Marshal Foch had already made it clear that the Rhine was "the only barrier which really assures the common defense of England, Belgium and France." All the more reason that the barrier not be abandoned before Germany had fulfilled the last condition of the treaty. Suppose, after the passage of sixteen or seventeen years, Germany had not defaulted on any of its annual installments and the Left bank had been evacuated. Suppose Germany had then fallen under the sway of a new imperialism and had suspended payments. What could France do in the form of reoccupation without great difficulty? Marshal Foch believed that defending the Rhine would require fewer troops than defending the proposed political frontier. Moreover, the Allies could always withdraw if they deemed it advisable. Poincaré said that he valued the proffered military alliance with Britain and America, but their aid, in event of German aggression, would not arrive in time. It would have no bearing, meanwhile, on obtaining the prompt and full payment of Germany's war indemnity. Therefore, the military alliance was no substitute for occupation, which he was sure the Allied and Associated governments would recognize. He was confident that they would concede to France the occupation, the one security indispensable for the payment of the debt.[54]

Clemenceau duly went through the motions of transmitting Poincaré's letter to Wilson and Lloyd George. The British Prime Minister replied on May 6, 1919, to the effect that his government had carefully considered President Poincaré's arguments, but that they still felt "that to compel the Germans to accept an Allied occupation of the Rhine for an indefinite period . . . would probably be a serious provocation [capable] of renewing tension and making Europe incur the risk of a new war." The British government thought that the Germans should be brought to understand that if they sincerely renounced "militaristic ambition," the Rhineland occupation would be maintained for only a reasonable length of time. Therefore, Britain could not consent to any change in the treaty recently drafted.[55]

In commenting upon Poincaré's letter, Lloyd George pointed out that the President of the Republic had directed his appeal to the economic interest of Britain and the United States, the two great banking and business communities. Lloyd George felt that Poincaré's letter was devious since "the whole of his argument . . . makes it clear that he was not thinking of a possession redeemable by the payment of debt, but that he contemplated a permanent occupation with the good will of the inhabitants of the Rhineland." [56]

President Wilson gave Poincaré's letter a polite brush-off. On May 9, 1919, he wrote Clemenceau that he had given full consideration to the letter from the President of the Republic. He had already heard the same reasoning from Marshal Foch. After weighing anew these arguments upon Clemenceau's request, he was still of the

---

[54] Poincaré's letter was published in full in *Le Temps,* September 12, 1921.

[55] Lloyd George's letter was published in French translation in *Le Temps,* September 13, 1921.

[56] Lloyd George, *The Truth,* I, 432; cf. Baker, *Woodrow Wilson and World Settlement,* II, 70.

opinion "that it would not be wise to go further than we have gone in the Treaty in respect to the occupation of the Rhine territory." [57]

President Poincaré's letter was briefly considered by the Council of Four, but, according to Lloyd George, "M. Clemenceau had already accepted our proposals and he never went back on an arrangement to which he had assented—however reluctantly." [58] This British testimony corroborates the viewpoint that Clemenceau had suggested to Poincaré that he write the letter only for appearance's sake, to mollify the President of the Republic and the marshal, and that the Tiger entertained no serious hope of persuading Wilson and Lloyd George to change the temporary occupation clauses. Clemenceau had told General Mordacq on April 24, four days before Poincaré's letter: "I will make no concessions on the treaty." [59] It is understandable why Foch and Poincaré suspected that Clemenceau was being less than candid with them. But Poincaré had done all that he felt he personally could do to modify the treaty.

Not so Marshal Foch, who did not share Poincaré's sense of political responsibility nor his inhibition in regard to a threat of resignation. Foch was all the more ready to make the threat when he learned that the treaty still provided for withdrawals from the Rhineland in three stages at five-year intervals. His British friend, Field Marshal Sir Henry Wilson, on April 28, confirmed the fact that the treaty retained the projected withdrawals. As Wilson expressed it, "Two hours with Foch, who is more maddened than ever with the Frocks. He tells me that the Tiger never sees him or tells him anything. I showed him the paper Hankey gave me last night, setting out that the Frocks contemplated armies of occupation for 15 years. . . . This was the first that Foch had heard of all this [60] and he and I got out the proposed new frontiers. It took us half an hour to find all the places, and to lay them out on the map. And all this

---

[57] Woodrow Wilson Papers, 1919, Library of Congress, Washington, D.C.
[58] Lloyd George, I, 43.
[59] Mordacq, *Le ministère Clemenceau,* III, 244.
[60] According to Recouly, Foch was complaining of the phased withdrawals at five-year intervals as early as April 15, 1919. See Recouly, *Le mémorial de Foch,* pp. 207–208.

has been done by the Frocks without Foch or me, or any soldier being consulted." [61] Foch's memory was elastic or defective in this incident; he had heard of the withdrawals, but he had not received official confirmation.

The marshal was goaded into writing an urgent letter to Clemenceau on May 5, with duplicate copies to President Wilson and Lloyd George. Foch declared that it was indispensable that the treaty be shown to him before its submission to the German delegation on May 7. He protested against certain "detestable" clauses which he "knew only in scraps." The marshal made it understood that, if these clauses were not modified, he would give his resignation as Commander-in-Chief of the Allied Armies.[62]

Before taking up Foch's ultimatum with President Wilson and Lloyd George, Clemenceau discussed it with General Mordacq. In utter weariness the Tiger said to his military adviser:

What I have seen in the course of this war! After having struggled for weeks and weeks, solely in the interests of my country, it is truly painful to receive such a letter from a man who has never wanted to understand that in order to make peace with Germany we can no more stand alone than when we were fighting her. Furthermore, he ought to recall that at the end of the war, when he was Commander-in-Chief, he had full authority to issue orders, yet he was not able to make himself obeyed by the Americans. In preparing a peace treaty I have no authority to give orders, but even so I have obtained about everything which one could get. What more does he want? [63]

Clemenceau added the comment that if he had frank relations with Poincaré the matter could be easily settled since the President of the Republic would ask Foch to withdraw his letter which was "deplorable from every point of view.... But in the present situation, what is to be done? For a fortnight Foch has been constantly at the Elysée. I question whether this letter has been written except after a close understanding between him and the President of the

[61] Charles E. Callwell, *Field-Marshal Sir Henry Wilson* (New York, 1927), II, 183.

[62] Mordacq, *Le ministère Clemenceau*, III, 259.

[63] Mordacq, III, 259.

Republic. In any case so much the worse for Foch, for I am obliged to act." [64]

This imbroglio was still another revelation of Clemenceau's consistent fault in regard to Foch—his secretiveness and disingenuousness. The Tiger was hardly the one entitled to tax Poincaré and Foch for want of frankness. He apparently regarded the marshal, not without cause, and, to a lesser degree, Poincaré, as incorrigibly stubborn and bullheaded. Consequently they were given only *pro forma* opportunities of repeating their views, when they insisted upon it. But Clemenceau made no serious effort to take his two foremost domestic antagonists into his confidence by candidly explaining to them the limitations upon his diplomatic choices, and then—but not before then—allowing the two doctrinaires to take his policy or leave it.

Prime Minister Clemenceau discussed Foch's ultimatum with President Wilson and Lloyd George. All three statesmen agreed that if Foch actually carried out his threat of resignation, he should be replaced at once by Marshal Pétain. Once again Pétain was informed of the possibility of his succeeding Foch.[65] But Foch did not actually resign since Clemenceau humored him once more by promising him one of the first copies of the treaty to come off the press, and by inviting him to speak freely before the plenary session of the Peace Conference which was to be held at the Ministry of Foreign Affairs the next day, May 6.

This last direct assault upon the Rhineland compromise was made twenty-four hours before the treaty draft was handed to the Germans. Foch was proud of his effort. As he explained to his admirer, Raymond Recouly: "I was brief, high strung, emphatic. The arguments were not so much advanced as pounded in by blows of the fist." [66] The marshal called the Conference's attention to the danger of the withdrawal from the Rhineland at the end of fifteen years. Reparation payments were to continue for thirty years, but the guarantees were to last for only fifteen. As for the right of reoccupying the

[64] Mordacq, III, 260.
[65] Mordacq, III, 260.
[66] Recouly, *Le mémorial de Foch*, p. 225.

Rhineland, that apparently was to be determined by the Reparation Commission, even if a hypothetical German infringement happened not to affect an indemnity clause of the treaty but rather a military or administrative clause. The treaty would offer complete safety only for the length of time that Germany would be harmless in any event—for five years. "As German power returns and our danger increases, our guarantees decrease." The marshal surprisingly proposed not occupation of the Rhineland, but only of the Rhine river itself. This would be the most economical and effective guarantee. The Rhine river should be held as long as a guarantee seemed necessary. France could at any time withdraw its troops if it so desired.[67]

Foch's swan song caused more surprise than emotion since most of his argument concerned indemnities, and financial policy was obviously outside the marshal's province. Moreover, he appeared to have shifted his ground from the plea for "annexation in disguise" which was implicit in his memorandum of November 27, 1918, even as he had abandoned the demands of January 10 and March 31, 1919 for "the occupation of the Rhine and of its strategic points while seeking a suitable political status for its inhabitants." All he now asked was military occupation of the river itself (and not even occupation of the Left bank hinterland) until all reparations had been paid.[68]

The marshal converted no one not already converted—he did not expect to do so, but as he viewed it, he was "freeing [himself] of responsibility for a treaty which [he] disapproved of in the strongest terms." [69]

Following Foch's address, the heads of the Allied governments met and decided to maintain the temporary occupation clauses of the treaty. Foch's persistent officiousness and interference in the

[67] See the report of P. W. Slosson, "Documentary History of the Treaty of Peace Between the Allied and Associated Powers and Germany," Part III, Section III, p. 2, in the Henry White Papers; cf. Tardieu, *The Truth About the Treaty,* pp. 189–193.

[68] Tardieu, p. 194; cf. Baker, *Woodrow Wilson and World Settlement,* II, 70.

[69] Recouly, p. 228.

normal functions of diplomacy had mystified the British. One of their delegates, Bonar Law, observed of Marshal Foch: "If a British general adopted such an attitude toward his government, he would not retain his post for five minutes." Clemenceau answered: "No matter how much I regret the attitude of the marshal, we cannot forget that he led our soldiers to victory." [70] There the matter rested.

Foch had all but lost his dogged campaign against the treaty, and was largely reduced henceforth to maneuvering with the Rhineland separatists themselves. The next day, May 7, the treaty draft was handed to the Germans for their consideration, which was to be prolonged seven weeks. Foch had thought of absenting himself from the ceremony as a silent protest, but after consultation with his chief of staff, General Weygand, he decided to attend. He was rewarded by the opportunity of observing sarcastically to Finance Minister Louis L. Klotz: "With the treaty you have just signed, sir, you can expect with certainty to be paid with monkey tricks." Klotz replied: "I am not in the habit of accepting such currency." To which Foch retorted: "Well, you'll be obliged to take it." [71] There was little left to Foch now except recrimination and some thoroughly questionable maneuvers behind the scenes to encourage Dr. Dorten and the other Rhineland separatists to carry off a coup which might confront the Versailles Conference with an accomplished fact before the final signing of the treaty in the Hall of Mirrors. A last twitch of determination was to be Foch's stratagem in exploiting the report of Germany's unwillingness to sign the treaty by using it as a pretext for dictating separate armistices to the component states of South Germany.

Perhaps the most judicious explanation of Marshal Foch's encroachment upon the formulation of French foreign policy is the verdict of Gabriel Terrail:

Since [Foch] had taken no part in discussing the solution which he regarded as so important, he, unlike our plenipotentiaries, did not know what a set purpose had been encountered with Lloyd George and Wilson.

[70] Tardieu, p. 195; cf. Mantoux, ed., *Les délibérations du conseil des quatre*, II, 410.

[71] Lhopital, *Foch, l'armistice et la paix*, p. 233.

. . . Viewing the question of the Left bank from the standpoint of strategy, and convinced that the security of France required a military frontier advanced to the Rhine, he regarded as inadequate the concessions which Clemenceau had wrested from our two Allies. This obstinacy of Marshal Foch was motivated only by his conception of the national interest. . . . He had no ulterior motives of a political nature.[72]

Clemenceau was no less aware than Foch of the strategic advantage of holding a river bank, with a glacis upon the other side. But, unlike Foch, and much of the French public whom he could not attempt to enlighten before the treaty's submission to Parliament for ratification, he perceived that France could enjoy the practical benefits of remotely controlling the Rhineland through its demilitarization, and through the right of its reoccupation in case of treaty infringement by Germany. Moreover, any such preclusive reoccupation by France would be done with Anglo-American concurrence rather than over their implacable opposition. Diplomacy is nearly always a gamble, and Clemenceau was gambling more wisely than Foch. The Tiger appreciated the considerable merit of Foch's strictly strategic point of view, and for this reason, quite as much as for caution in domestic politics, he treated the marshal's arrogation and insubordination with leniency and magnanimity.

[72] Terrail, *Le combat des trois,* pp. 223–224.

Chapter IV

The Palatinate-Rhineland Putsch

As a sort of mockery of Marshal Foch's hopes, there blew up toward the end of May 1919 the noisy and nugatory Palatinate-Rhineland Rebellion. It was a ludicrous imbroglio replete with plots and counter-plots, with scurrying Palatine and Rhenish conspirators abetted by the French military, and with mystified and indignant American and British authorities protesting against suspected skulduggery. Nearly everyone seemed to want to enter the act—Gérard, Mangin, Dorten, the chemist Eberhard Haas, Clemenceau, Foch, President Wilson and his Rhineland occupation commanders, Generals Liggett and Allen. Marshal Foch lurked mostly off stage, but in this farce he was as much impresario as accessory.

After the draft of the Treaty of Versailles had been submitted to the German delegation on May 7, it was as obvious to Marshal Foch and Generals Mangin and Gérard as to Dr. Dorten that, if there was to be a Rhineland freed from Prussian control, or a Palatinate freed from Bavaria, it could only be as a result of self-liberation by the inhabitants, abetted by the French, and possibly recognized belatedly as an accomplished fact by the Peace Conference. This was a slender hope, but the disclosure of the severe peace terms caused dismay in Germany, which redounded, at least temporarily, to the advantage of the separatists. General Liggett's successor as the American occupation commander, General Henry T. Allen, was told by Walter Rathenau (who, as President of Allgemeine Elektrizitäts-Gesellschaft, had numerous German business connections) that the heavy war indemnities imposed by the treaty convinced many large industrialists of the Rhineland and Westphalia that an autonomous state would be the best way to lighten their reparations burdens.[1] However, the association of separatism with the large industrialists alienated the Social Democratic working class, already in a mood of rebellion against the pillars of society since the loss of the war.

The catalytic agent of separatism in the Bavarian Palatinate was the alarming news of the seizure of Munich by the Spartacists in May 1919, following the assassination of Kurt Eisner, the Minority Socialist politician who had presided over a mildly revolutionary regime in Bavaria for several months. Numerous conservative Catholics and Centrists in the Palatinate wanted to cut the governmental ties binding their Bavarian exclave with a Munich now in the grip of rabid Spartacists.[2]

There was a sanguine belief nurtured by some Rhinelanders and Palatines that the formation of one or more autonomous republics in West Germany could confer a great diplomatic benefit upon Germany as a whole. If these new states were sanctioned by immediate plebiscites and were represented at the Versailles Conference by delegations, they might obtain an alleviation of the treaty's burdens for all of Germany. If the Allies were confronted with the tempting bait of a Western-oriented, autonomous Rhenish Republic and a Palatine Republic, they might be induced to relax their hard demands for the cession of the border territories of Eupen, Malmédy, Danzig, and the Saar. Prussia and Bavaria would have to defer to Germany's overriding interests and restrain their anger at the thought of losing their Rhenish and Palatine exclaves, which would become autonomous republics within the Reich. The military occupation of Germany might be greatly lightened or perhaps might even disappear altogether; France and Belgium would win sincere friends in the Palatinate and Rhineland; all of the Germans would be happy to retain their border territories, albeit in autonomous states incor-

[1] Henry T. Allen, *The Rhineland Occupation* (Indianapolis, 1927), pp. 189–190.

[2] Erwin Goebel, *Die pfälzische Presse im Abwehrkampf der Pfalz gegen Franzosen und Separatisten 1918–1924* (Ludwigshafen, 1931), pp. 34–35, 86, 89–90.

porated within the Reich; and there would be general rejoicing over reduced reparations. Such was the gossamer web of separatist aspirations in May 1919.[3]

The first effort to realize these reveries occurred in the Bavarian Palatinate. In complete independence of Dr. Dorten and General Mangin, twenty-one Palatine "notables" were abetted by General Gérard, commander of the Eighth Army with headquarters at Landau, in their designs of setting up an autonomous republic. Without consulting Mangin in the least, General Gérard intervened with the Bavarian governor of the province of Spire, Administrative President von Winterstein, to demand an audience for the Palatine "notables." Von Winterstein replied to Gérard that he would receive the delegation with good will, and that he would see what was to be done about their wishes.[4] He admitted the delegation on May 17 and heard their demands for independence from Bavaria, which could be achieved by convoking a new popular assembly.[5] Von Winterstein would agree only to the convocation of the Landrat, in which the separatists had no confidence. This provincial council, with its old wartime membership of conservatives, met the next day and pronounced unanimously in favor of retaining the Palatinate within the framework of Germany, and it asked also for the retention of the Saarland.[6] These modest desiderata hardly amounted to the separatist demand for an autonomous Palatine Republic within the Reich.

Seeing that they would get nowhere with the cautious Landrat, the separatists decided to act upon their own reponsibility, relying upon General Gérard's patronage. On the night of May 20, 1919, an unsigned proclamation was posted throughout the Palatinate calling upon its inhabitants to form a new republic to be linked by a customs

[3] Guy de Traversay, "La première tentative de République rhénane," *La Revue de Paris* (December 1, 1928), p. 589.

[4] Vial-Mazel, *Erreurs et oublis de Georges Clemenceau*, p. 86.

[5] See article by Administrative President von Winterstein, "Der 18 Mai 1919, ein Gedenktag der pfälzischen Geschichte," in *Dokumente aus dem Befreiungskampf der Pfalz*, Pfälzische Rundschau 1930, pp. 5–7. For a reproduction of a handbill opposing the Frei Pfalz Committee, see above p. 9. See also Brüggemann, *Die Rheinische Republik*, pp. 105–106.

[6] Vial-Mazel, p. 85; cf. *Frankfurter Zeitung*, May 22, 1919.

union with the Saar. It said in part: "There will be three frontiers—a political frontier, a military frontier, and a tariff frontier. There is but one road to safety from this [desperate] situation: formation of an independent neutral state without loss of territory, with economic union with the Saar Basin. We desire to remain German throughout—German institutions, German customs, German administration." [7]

This revolutionary exhortation met with a lackadaisical response in Speyer, Landau, and in Zweibrücken in the Saar, where there were some fitful demonstrations. However, there was certainly no discernible separatist ground swell. Administrative President von Winterstein noted the apathetic response and sprang a trap upon four of the most important leaders of the movement. He had the prosecutor of Landau, Herr Heuck, obtain orders for their arrest from Judge Kammerer, which were to be executed by the mayor of Landau, Herr Mahla. On May 21 the ringleader, the biochemist Dr. Eberhard Haas, two businessmen, the lumberman Hofer and the rug merchant Schenk, and an architect, Müller, were arrested. Their residences were searched and their separatist tracts seized. [8]

The French riposte was immediate. Notifying Foch of what he was about to do, General Gérard demanded the immediate release of the four "notables" and the return of their separatist propaganda. Mayor Mahla, Judge Kammerer, and Prosecutor Heuck were jailed in their turn. After a preliminary investigation at Spire in which the duplicity of Administrative President von Winterstein was revealed in the arrests of the separatists, General Gérard ordered the expulsion from occupied territory of the perfidious provincial governor, despite his pleas of innocence. Von Winterstein was soon packed off, and General Gérard issued a proclamation on May 22, 1919, to reassure the separatists of France's benevolence and protection. It read as follows:

[7] Quoted in Allen, *The Rhineland Occupation*, p. 191.
[8] *Dokumente aus dem Befreiungskampf der Pfalz*, pp. 31–32; cf. Robert Oberhauser, *Kampf der Westmarck*, p. 49; cf. Vial-Mazel, p. 87; cf. Jacquot, *General Gérard und die Pfalz*, pp. 114–115; see also *Kölnische Zeitung*, May 21, 1919; and *Frankfurter Zeitung*, May 23, 1919.

Inhabitants of Landau have been molested by certain German functionaries because of their sympathies for France.

Such acts on the part of functionaries constitute an abuse of power, a disregard for the orders of Marshal Foch, and an inconvenience for victorious and benevolent France. Sanctions have been invoked against these aforesaid functionaries.

The French military authority has always abstained from taking part in any political propaganda whatsoever. It is exclusively concerned with the well-being of the citizenry and the workers, and it has the firm intention of safeguarding the [population] from terrorist influence, and enabling it to express its wishes freely in regard to the greatest good and prosperity of their country, upon the sole condition that there be no disturbance of public order, for which the French Army is responsible.

Therefore, the Commander of the Army wants to reassure honest citizens that they will be protected against those who place their personal interests above the general interests of the populace.[9]

The French occupation authorities, with Marshal Foch's full benediction, were trying to have it both ways with regard to the separatist movement. While formally proclaiming that they were "taking no part whatsoever in political propaganda," they were moving heaven and earth to incite the separatists to bring off a coup.

The German government's reaction to General Gérard's efforts at subornation was as instantaneous as might have been expected. The head of the German delegation of the Armistice Commission at Spa, General von Hammerstein, voiced the following protest:

The French Commander-in-Chief of the Palatinate, General Gérard, and the French authorities under him, have undertaken by misuse of their rights under the armistice agreement, to promote and support [a] revolution which has [as its goal] the separation of the Palatinate from Bavaria and from Germany. The attempt to proclaim an independent republic of the Palatinate and the forceful separation of this political unit from Bavaria and from Germany, has been initiated by twenty one persons. The great majority of the inhabitants of the Palatinate, stirred and excited by treasonable acts of these persons, are convinced that their

[9] *Frankfurter Zeitung,* May 25, 1919; cf. Vial-Mazel, pp. 89–90; see also Paul Grossman, *Im Kampf um den Rhein 1918–1930* (Frankfurt am Main, 1933), p. 17.

leaders have been influenced by low and materialistic motives.

At the present time when the plenipotentiaries of the German government and the Allied and Associated governments are assembled in Versailles for the purpose of bringing about a conclusion of peace, the German government cannot conceive of so flagrant a violation of self-determination as that of General Gérard, in which he has the approval of the Commander-in-Chief of the Allied Armies, Marshal Foch, and that of the French government.[10]

The German government demanded that General Gérard be relieved of his command immediately.[11]

The *coryphées* of the second act of the separatist comedy were General Mangin and Dr. Dorten, who were completely out of step with Gérard and his conspiratorial chemist, Dr. Haas. Mangin even surpassed General Gérard in trying to egg on the separatists while coyly professing "neutrality" in German politics; but, incredible to relate, the two French generals did not coördinate any of their conspiratorial efforts. Dorten had been expecting great things of General Mangin ever since he gained belated access to his headquarters at Mainz in April 1919. Dorten wanted Mangin to make the acquaintance of the leaders of the committees of the North, who had no connections with the Palatine plotters. The committees of the North had been operating from Aachen since the defection of Konrad Adenauer, the mayor of Cologne. General Mangin was planning a trip to Aachen, in the Belgian zone, in the second week of May, to take command of an army corps. Dorten wanted Mangin to meet Bertram Kastert, the vicar of Sainte-Colomba and a Centrist Deputy of the Reichstag, but the suddenness of the general's trip caused a postponement of that pleasure. Consequently, Mangin met only minor separatists in the North.[12]

One of these spear bearers made a favorable impression upon the general, who described him as "a simple postal employee, intelligent,

---

[10] Quoted in American Military Government of Occupied Germany, 1918–1920, Report of Officer in Charge of Civil Affairs, I, 388, in the Henry T. Allen Papers, 1919, Library of Congress, Washington, D.C.

[11] General Nudant, "A Spa: journal du président de la commission interallié d'armistice (1918–1919)," *La Revue de France* (April 1, 1925), p. 493; cf. *Frankfurter Zeitung*, May 23, 1919.

[12] Dorten, *La tragédie rhénane*, p. 66.

with a physiognomy more Roman than Germanic." The general listened attentively to the separatist's familiar plan of an autonomous Rhineland within the framework of the Reich. Mangin expressed sympathetic interest, but then without further ado proceeded to set the postal employee upon the right track.

The Entente ignores the Rhinelanders [Mangin explained], and the treaty speaks only of Germany. . . . If the Rhinelanders want a special status in the German Republic, it is to Germany that they will have to address themselves. This is the point of view of the Entente. . . .

All, then, is lost if [the Rhinelanders] adhere to their present intentions.

But all could be saved if, instead of demanding a republic constituting a part of Germany, they strove for an *independent* republic.[13] The severance from Berlin ought to be complete. Then you could rely upon the Wilsonian principle of the self-determination of peoples. An autonomous, German republic, you say; add to it *independent,* and demand the right of being represented at the Versailles Conference. . . . I speak for myself, for the Entente has such scruples that it will give its representatives no intructions, so the greatest freedom is left to you. Understand that [the Entente] regards you as reasonable men (although I think that you are still children), and as citizens (although you are still subjects, allow me to say to you). But if there are . . . leaders among you, men of action who . . . can be men of thought, this is the time for them to . . . activate the inert masses.[14]

The separatists of Aachen were delighted with such fire-breathing encouragement from General Mangin. They responded with alacrity to his invitation to work with Dorten in preparing a project which Mangin would submit to the French government. They decided to send a delegation to the general's headquarters at Mainz for further refinement of their plans. The delegation was to be headed by the redoubtable vicar-politician, Bertram Kastert. It was also to include another ecclesiastic, Dr. Joseph Frohberger of Bonn, the editor of the *Kölnische Volkszeitung,* whose reliability was soon to be questioned by the others.[15]

Meanwhile, General Mangin prepared a gala reception for Mar-

---

[13] Italics Mangin's.

[14] General Charles Mangin, "Lettres de Rhénanie," p. 514; cf. Major Louis Mangin, *La France et le Rhin,* pp. 47–50.

[15] Dorten, p. 67.

shal Foch upon his return to his Mainz headquarters. On May 13, 1919, the marshal was received by three battalions of Senegalese, three battalions of troops from metropolitan France, and a squadron of red-caped Spahis mounted on white horses. Following a ceremonial dinner there was a torchlight parade, and the evening's entertainment culminated in fireworks.[16] During his two days at Mainz the marshal had ample opportunity to be briefed upon all the prospects of Rhineland separatism. Although Clemenceau claimed that Mangin told him nothing of his numerous conversations with Dorten,[17] Marshal Foch was hardly in such a state of ignorance.[18]

The time approached for the visit to General Mangin of the delegation from the Committees of the North, representing separatists in Aachen and Rhenish Nassau-Hesse. Dorten conferred with Bertram Kastert and with another Rhineland Centrist Deputy, Herr Kuckhoff, as well as Frohberger. After laborious deliberation, the four separatist leaders drew up a plan to show General Mangin. It was understood that Mangin wanted a completely independent Rhineland state, whereas Dorten wanted an autonomous state within the Reich. The draft proposed a monstrosity—a Rhenish state *within* the Reich, and yet free to act in its own interests *outside* the Reich. This strange, new political entity would have its own diplomatic representation which would be empowered to treat directly with the Allies on all matters concerning the occupation of its territory.[19]

The separatist leaders agreed that the proclamation of their state would be issued May 24 from Coblenz, which was to be its capital. It was assumed that placing the capital in the American zone would conceal the French influence.[20] They agreed further to set up a provisional Rhenish government which would serve only long enough

---

[16] General Charles Mangin, "Lettres de Rhénanie," p. 516.

[17] Clemenceau, *Grandeur and Misery*, p. 214.

[18] Major Louis Mangin, *La France et le Rhin*, pp. 39–42; cf. Baker, *Woodrow Wilson and World Settlement*, II, 85.

[19] Dorten, *La tragédie rhénane*, pp. 67–68.

[20] Baker, II, 86.

to prepare a plebiscite, the procedure of which would be submitted to the Peace Conference by an ad hoc delegation.[21] The Rhenish state would not attempt to evade reparations, but its special delegation would try to win concessions for all of Germany from the Peace Conference—an act of intercession which would make Germany much more likely to accept the new state. The ambitious republic was to comprise at least Rhenish Prussia, Rhenish Hesse, the Bavarian Palatinate, and Old Nassau—territories having no less than twelve million inhabitants.[22] There was an intimation that it might include the Saarland as well.

General Mangin received the separatist leaders at his headquarters on May 17, 1919. The group numbered ten, including Dorten, and the deputies Kastert and Kuckhoff. Frohberger served as spokesman, with Dorten acting as interpreter. Mangin agreed to ask the American authorities to allow the conspirators to issue their proclamation in Coblenz, which was the American occupation headquarters.[23] But Mangin told the delegation that only the Peace Conference could commit itself on the Rhenish state; that the treaty had already been elaborated by all the Allies and it was not likely to be changed; that, moreover, the Conference would not find it possible to enter into relations with the Rhinelanders unless they confronted the Conference with the *fait accompli* of asserted sovereignty.[24]

Clemenceau contended that Mangin went so far as to pronounce the original Rhineland republic program "unacceptable." [25] Mangin hints at this in his account of the meeting, which follows:

Mainz, 17 May 1919

This afternoon a three hour conference with the Rhineland Republic Committee. The question is not resolved. The hour has passed for presenting themselves to the Peace Conference as a new state, and the

[21] Dorten, p. 68.

[22] Aulneau, *Le Rhin et la France,* p. 278.

[23] Dorten, *La tragédie rhénane,* p. 68; cf. *Die Gruende,* p. 42; see also Brüggemann, *Die Rheinische Republik,* p. 99.

[24] Aulneau, p. 278; Brüggemann, pp. 101–102.

[25] Clemenceau, *Grandeur and Misery,* p. 217; cf. Grimm, *Poincaré am Rhein,* p. 25.

leaders are very timid. They claim that the time has not yet come to proclaim independence, and they are content to try to fit into the framework of the German Reich. They lay claim to the Saar, which I tell them cannot be allowed. The Saar will decide for itself at a suitable time. But this would be the opportunity for them to achieve their autonomy while remaining German. It is very interesting, but a much slower development than I hoped for at Aachen.[26]

Dr. Dorten promised to prepare another draft for Mangin, which would meet his objections in regard to claiming the Saar.[27] This Dorten did on May 21. Mangin then had no further objection, seeing that there was no allusion to the Saar, although he was still dissatisfied over the intention to proclaim an autonomous rather than an independent state.[28]

Clemenceau, in commenting upon this "partnership," made the following mild observation:

What becomes, in all this, of that *strict neutrality* which, for the head of an army of occupation, is the paramount duty? And all the time, at the Peace Conference, I was fighting to obtain the occupation of the Left bank of the Rhine for five, ten, fifteen years, and I was saying to England and America, "Don't be alarmed, we have not the slightest thought of annexation." Has a soldier, then, a right to involve his government in such an adventure without informing them of it? It was only too easy to read in this "collaboration" of General Mangin with Dorten an enterprise capable of preparing the disintegration of Germany and the "integration" of the Rhineland with French territory.[29]

Clemenceau was again caught in a crossfire between Allied opposition to a truncated Germany, and French public opinion which demanded it as indicated by the flood of books on the proposal. The French military knew quite well that they were strongly supported by popular sentiment at home in their determination to fracture Germany. A further psychological handicap for Clemenceau

---

[26] General Charles Mangin, "Lettres de Rhénanie," p. 517.
[27] Clemenceau, p. 218.
[28] General Charles Mangin, "Lettres de Rhénanie," p. 518.
[29] Clemenceau, p. 218.

was the known fact that originally he, too, had wanted a detached Rhineland, and was compelled to abandon that objective only when he saw that it meant the loss of France's indispensable allies. The Tiger could not summarily remove his scheming, recalcitrant military such as Foch, Mangin, and Gérard, without enraging the French electorate and thereby endangering the chances of Parliament's ratification of the entire treaty. Clemenceau's Fabian tactics toward the French military caused some of the members of the American peace delegation, especially Ray Stannard Baker, to suspect that he was in collusion with them in their tireless plotting.[30] There was, of course, no factual basis for this assumption. What the record does reveal is that Clemenceau reproved his generals as if they were only wayward sons whom he fully understood and readily forgave for their excessive animal spirits. An American or British head of state would probably have sacked them on the spot, and without the faintest misgiving or compunction. But it would have required no heroism, since Anglo-American national conditioning would have permitted—even required—it.

Word of the separatists' conference with Mangin, and even the text of the compromise draft which had been submitted to the general, were transmitted by the perfidious Frohberger to the British at Cologne, and to Captain Schwenk, the German liaison officer at British headquarters, who immediately warned Philipp Scheidemann, the President of the Prussian Council.[31] Scheidemann was thus in a position to prepare counter measures to crush any separatist *putsch*. With almost pathetic optimism, the two deputies who were members of Dorten's delegation to Mangin, Kastert and Kuckhoff, offered to go to Berlin to notify personally the two-score Rhenish deputies of the impending coup to enable them to leave the Prussian capital in time to join the movement in the Rhineland.

Soon after Kastert and Kuckhoff arrived in Berlin Scheidemann

---

[30] Baker, *Woodrow Wilson and World Settlement,* II, 88–89; see also Gedye, *The Revolver Republic,* p. 46.

[31] Dorten, *La tragédie rhénane,* p. 69; cf. *Kölnische Zeitung,* May 28, 1919; see also Gedye, p. 68.

released his counterattack. He issued a warning to all the Rhenish deputies to take no part in any separatist movement.[32] He sent Social Democratic agitators into the laboring districts to foment working-class opposition to separatism. On May 25, 1919, the *Rheinisch-Westfälische Zeitung* of Essen published a deceptively succinct account of the visit of the delegates to General Mangin, giving the impression that the separatists wanted to create a buffer state by cutting the ties not only with Prussia but also with Germany. The final blow was Scheidemann's order to all functionaries to publish a warning that any separatist movement would be prosecuted as high treason, and in accordance with Article 81 of the penal code those taking part in such a conspiracy would be subject to penal servitude or imprisonment for life.[33] The naive but resolute conspirators, Kastert and Kuckhoff, thereupon relinquished their mandates as deputies and returned to Cologne to resume the struggle with Dorten and Mangin.[34]

General Mangin was trying, meanwhile, to carry out his promise of assistance to Dorten. On May 22 he recorded in his journal the following entry:

I have sent General Denvignes to my American neighbor [General Hunter Liggett] to learn his intentions in regard to the Rhenish Republic which they want to proclaim from [the American zone], for Coblenz will be the future capital. He indicated to me that he is personally quite favorable, and he wants to be of assistance to me in advancing France's interests. But he has orders to oppose all changes in the government. Thus forewarned, I communicated with the principal leader [Dorten], who, although checked, demands to go to Coblenz to forestall a Prussian counter blow which is being prepared. Thierry [a colonel on Mangin's staff in the Tenth Army] yesterday spoke with the British from whom I shall obtain, I believe, at least negative agreement. It is piquant

32 *Rheinisch-Westfälische Zeitung*, May 29, 1919.

33 *Rheinisch-Westfälische Zeitung*, May 29, 1919; cf. Dorten, pp. 69–70; see also Clemenceau, *Grandeur and Misery*, pp. 214–215; also *Die Gruende*, p. 42; also *Le Temps*, June 5, 1919.

34 Dorten, "The Rhineland Movement," p. 404; cf. *L'Echo de Paris*, June 2, 1919; see also *Kölnische Zeitung*, May 31, 1919.

to see free America opposing an expression of popular sentiment: it is simply a question of convoking a Constituent [Assembly] here.[35]

The Americans had a confused idea as to exactly who the separatists were, and what they were planning to do. General Hunter Liggett, the American Commander of the Third Army of Occupation on the Rhine, reported that at Coblenz

. . . on May 22nd, a delegation of French officers from Mayence . . . waited upon me and said that it was understood at Mayence that the Rhenish Republic was to be established; that fifty delegates would soon meet at Coblenz and establish a German Independent State with a new set of civil officers; that the French Commander on the Rhine was prepared to recognize the new Civil Government to be set up at Coblenz and was anxious to know what we would do. I informed them that we had no authority to acquiesce in any such plan for a meeting of delegates at Coblenz; that under existing instructions we should decline to deal with any new government and would recognize only the one existing; that if they expected anything else they should go to Treves, the Advance American General Headquarters.[36]

General Liggett's political adviser, Pierrepont B. Noyes, the American Rhineland Commissioner from April 1919 to June 1920, was apparently mystified by the statement of the French spokesman that "fifty officials of the new administration were then on their way to Coblenz to organize the government. . . . We found that fifty billets had been actually engaged for the Dorten officials by the French Mission in Coblenz, and it turned out that carloads of proclamations had been printed and were ready for distribution." [37] Noyes leapt to the bizarre conclusion that Mangin and Dorten were sending French deputies to Coblenz to proclaim "Rhineland independence!" [38] When Noyes's skewed version

---

[35] General Charles Mangin, "Lettres de Rhénanie," p. 518.

[36] Hunter Liggett, *Commanding an American Army* (Boston, 1925), pp. 141–143.

[37] Pierrepont B. Noyes, *While Europe Waits for Peace* (New York, 1921), pp. 55–56.

[38] Dorten, *La tragédie rhénane*, p. 70.

reached General Pershing and President Wilson, the American chieftains must have doubted the very sanity of the French.

General Henry T. Allen, who in July 1919 was to replace General Liggett, had the same uncertainty in regard to the nationality of the fifty deputies. He wrote in his book, *The Rhineland Occupation*, that "General Mangin was informed that we must refuse to recognize revolutionary movements of any character, and that if workers for a Rhenish republic entered the American area, regardless of whether they be of *French* [39] or German nationality, they would be treated on the same basis as other agitators." [40] Things were indeed going badly for Dorten, Mangin, and Foch when the Americans were led to believe, even if only momentarily, that the French were so incorrigible in their expansionist intentions toward Germany that they could actually think of sending French deputies from Paris to Coblenz to proclaim a Rhenish republic. The Americans were obviously lost in the terra incognita of European diplomacy, but they were no more novices than Dorten, Mangin, and Foch, with their vision of a toy state in the Rhineland, where friendly spirits would dwell forever in harmonious relations with both France and Germany.

Belatedly aware of the need of adequate information on the impending rebellion, the Civil Affairs Officer of the Third American Army, Colonel I. L. Hunt, summoned the chief municipal councilor of Coblenz, Dr. Brandt, and "without intimating in any way that the French were behind the movement," he requested Prussian officials in the American zone to begin an investigation of the plot. Colonel Hunt supplied Dr. Brandt with Denvignes' list of the names of Dorten's tentative "cabinet members" including, in addition to "Premier" Dorten himself, President Wallraff of Aachen, Minister of Interior Stegerwalt of Mainz, Minister of Finance Hagen of Cologne, Minister of Justice Fuld of Mainz, Minister of Agriculture Buhl of Diedesheim in the Palatinate, and Minister of Education Kuckhoff of Cologne. [41] Dr. Brandt complied with Colonel

---

[39] Italics mine.

[40] Allen, *The Rhineland Occupation*, pp. 193–194.

[41] Report of I. L. Lunt, Colonel, Infantry, Officer in Charge, Civil Affairs,

Hunt's request, and the municipal councilor shortly reported that he had seen the cleric Frohberger who had told him everything which the separatists had done so far and planned to do in the future.[42]

But before Frohberger's accurate version of the conspiracy could be disseminated, the American military and civilian chiefs had received a garbled account of the plot which was recorded in General John J. Pershing's diary for May 22, the day Mangin sent his officers to see General Liggett:

> When I returned to the office after luncheon I received a communication from General Liggett . . . to the effect: that this morning one of the members of General Mangin's staff called on General Liggett for the purpose of knowing what our attitude would be toward a political revolution on the West bank of the Rhine. . . . The Colonel wished to know if General Liggett would do business with the new government and if he would allow the French to send fifty agitators, on May 24th, into the area controlled by the American Army of Occupation for the purpose of assisting this political revolution. General Liggett of course refused to permit the entry of these agitators without instructions from me. After verifying this report I advised General Eltinge to tell General Liggett that I approved the action he had taken. . . . This evening I wrote a letter to the President enclosing a copy of this communication and informing him of the action taken.[43]

President Wilson addressed a letter to Clemenceau on May 23, quoting Pershing's message, and adding his own comment for the Tiger's benefit: "General Liggett very properly declined to consider the proposition, and his action has my entire approval. He has given instructions not to permit the entry of political agitators into our sector no matter by whose order they may claim to be operating, and I feel confident that these orders meet with your own approval."[44]

Clemenceau had been placed in an acutely embarrassing position

---

Headquarters Third Army, in the Tasker H. Bliss Papers; cf. *Kölnische Zeitung,* May 28, 1919.

[42] *Kölnische Zeitung,* May 28, 1919.

[43] John J. Pershing Papers, 1919, Library of Congress, Washington, D.C.

[44] Woodrow Wilson Papers, 1919, Library of Congress, Washington, D.C.

by his gauche military. His American critic, Ray Stannard Baker, who suspected him of at least moral complicity in the Rhine rebellion—incitement of thought, if not of word or deed—conceded that "Clemenceau's course was entirely correct" in what followed.[45] As soon as the Tiger received Wilson's polite but appalling letter he instructed Jules Jeanneney, the Under-Secretary of State to the President of the Council, to go to Germany at once to find out what the French generals had been doing. On May 24 Jeanneney interviewed Generals Fayolle and Mangin at their Mainz headquarters. On the following day he went to Coblenz where he questioned Denvignes, Mangin's emissary to General Liggett. Jeanneney then held a conference with General Liggett himself, and before returning to Paris he went back to Mainz to see Mangin again.[46] Mangin admitted that his "liaison officer had perhaps exceeded his instructions somewhat, but in the last analysis he had fulfilled his mission by informing my American colleague and by asking his intentions." [47] On May 26 Jeanneney prepared a report which he submitted at once to Clemenceau.

The Under-Secretary of State removed the veil of mystery from the plot. He assured the Tiger that the fifty deputies who were to have been sent to Coblenz on May 24 were to have been German, not French. The Rhine republic was to be German, freed only from Prussia. General Mangin had indeed sent Denvignes to General Liggett on a briefing mission, and moreover he had sent a second officer to Cologne to explain the project to the British occupation commander, General Robertson, and a third emissary to Aachen to inform the Belgian commander, General Michel.[48] Jeanneney concluded his report with an account of the frequent conferences which Mangin had held with the promoters of separatism.[49]

Since all the conspiratorial cats had been prematurely let out of

---

[45] Baker, *Woodrow Wilson and World Settlement,* II, 89.

[46] Clemenceau, *Grandeur and Misery,* p. 216; cf. Major Louis Mangin, *La France et le Rhin,* p. 53.

[47] General Charles Mangin, "Lettres de Rhénanie," p. 519.

[48] Clemenceau, p. 217.

[49] Clemenceau, p. 218.

the bag as the consequence of Mangin's sending Denvignes to General Liggett, the separatists naturally had to change their plans. Some delay was now inevitable. Using the American or British zone of occupation as the place for proclaiming the republic now was ruled out, but there remained the Belgian zone—and, as a last resort, the French zone. Dr. Dorten and Bertram Kastert summoned the delegates of all the united committees to a meeting to be held May 29, 1919, in the Imperial Hall of Charlemagne's Palace in Aachen.

Dorten visited Mangin on May 25, the day after Jeanneney had questioned the general. Mangin approved the idea of proclaiming the republic from Aachen, since Cologne and Coblenz were unavailable for that purpose. Dorten claimed that Mangin said to him that "in his opinion, an action in the Belgian zone, not directly involving France, would permit the French government to declare itself in our favor." Dorten contended further that "without informing me in detail of the [Jeanneney] conversation, the general assured me that Clemenceau had allowed him to pursue his goal." The general said to Dorten, "You see, politicians are always happy when they can evade responsibility; they do not want historical records." [50] This reconstruction of Dorten's is credible. Mangin, knowing Clemenceau's original support of a detached Rhineland, and taking his long silence for tacit consent, assumed that the Tiger would not really object to being confronted with the accomplished fact of a Rhineland republic. We do not know exactly what Jeanneney said to Mangin, but as an interrogator he probably asked questions, allowing the general to do the explaining. Dorten's claims do not convict Clemenceau of duplicity: whatever his original concurrence in separatism, the Tiger was no confederate of the blundering generals who placed him and France in a ridiculous light with relation to the Allies. [51]

The separatists encountered one setback after another. Encouraged once more by Mangin, Dorten visited Aachen in the belief that

[50] Dorten, *La tragédie rhénane,* pp. 71, 77; cf. Guy de Traversay, "La première tentative de République rhénane," pp. 592–593.

[51] Guy de Traversay, p. 593.

the mayor of the city and the Belgian authorities would put the City Hall at his disposal. Dorten went to Belgian headquarters where he was told, gently but firmly, that he would not be allowed to proclaim his republic from that zone. Moreover, on May 28 the Prussian Prefect notified the Belgians that a general strike would paralyze Aachen the moment the separatists undertook their coup. Dorten learned that labor leaders had actually arrived in Aachen from Cologne to conduct the strike. The separatists suspected that the British, acting upon Prussian demands, had brought pressure to bear upon the Belgians to frustrate the plotters. Shortly before, an English ordinance had been posted in Cologne, which spelled out London's hostility to the Rhine rebellion. It read as follows:

The authorities of His British Majesty make known to the population inhabiting the zone occupied by the British troops that no change in the German constitution will be permitted in the Rhineland, and that no new authority will assume office for the entire duration of the British occupation, except with the previous consent of England.

All persons transgressing this ordinance or assisting in violation thereof will be punished with imprisonment or expulsion or both penalties.

[Signed:] G. S. Clive
Major General, British Military Governor
Occupied German Territory[52]

Once again the conspirators were discomfited by Dr. Frohberger, who had informed the British and the Prussian governments of the latest evolution of the plot.[53]

It was only later that Dorten perceived that a deep-seated contrariety of interest precluded a common Rhenish policy on the part of Britain, France, and Belgium. Britain—and, naturally, Germany—wanted above all else to prevent French domination of the Rhenish-Westphalian industrial regions. If all the Rhineland were included in a detached state which was oriented toward Paris, it would confer a great economic advantage upon the French metallurgical industry, which would be opposed by Britain, Belgium, and Ger-

---

[52] Translated from quotation in Dorten, p. 72; cf. Weymar, *Konrad Adenauer*, pp. 80–81; see also Binoux, *La question rhénane et la France*, pp. 74–75; also Brüggemann, *Die Rheinische Republik*, pp. 109–110, 113–114.

[53] Dorten, *La tragédie rhénane*, p. 73.

many. "A fusion of Rhenish coal with French ore would lead to a coalition of heavy industry [which could] dominate the European market." [54]

Dorten was hard to discourage, but he felt daunted after having learned of the fiasco of General Gérard and Dr. Haas in the Palatinate on May 22, as well as the ludicrous results of the Denvignes mission to General Liggett, and now the manifestations of Belgian and British hostility to separatism. He was almost ready to call off proclaiming the Rhineland republic, which appeared unattainable against such odds. When he met, as planned, with the chiefs of the united committees at Aachen on May 29, one more item of disturbing news was brought to his attention. In the Palatinate, Dr. Haas was preparing another coup. Ever since the Bavarian Administrative President von Winterstein had ordered the arrest of chemist Haas and the other Palatine "notables," Dorten had considered the Palatinate Republic movement *hors de combat*.[55] His Rhineland movement had established no connections whatsoever with the more restricted Palatinate conspiracy of Dr. Haas and General Gérard. Dorten's grandiose republic was supposed to inglobe not only Rhenish Prussia, Rhenish Hesse, and Old Nassau, but also the Bavarian Palatinate. Obviously Dorten and Haas, now that the chemist's release from jail had been effected by General Gérard, would be working at cross purposes if Haas planned still another bid for power after the piddling performance of the Palatine separatists at Landau, Speyer, and Zweibrucken on May 22, 1919.

It was one of Dorten's loyal chiefs of committees, a Centrist from the Palatinate, Dr. Wuelk, who alerted the Aachen meeting with the report that at Landau, in General Gérard's zone of occupation, Dr. Haas' Freie Pfalz committee was being reactivated for the purpose of creating an independent state which would be restricted to the Palatinate—the original plan of Haas and General Gérard. According to Wuelk, the "majority" of the residents of the Palati-

---

[54] Dorten, "The Rhineland Movement," p. 404; cf. Bruno Kuske, *Rheingrenze und Pufferstaat* (Bonn, 1919), p. 5; also Gedye, *The Revolver Republic,* p. 76.

[55] Guy de Traversay, "La première tentative de République rhénane," p. 589.

nate opposed this scheme, preferring their province's inclusion in Dorten's much more capacious Rhineland republic.[56]

Wuelk's thunderbolt galvanized Dorten's followers, ending all their irresolution. They could not stand by and allow Haas and General Gérard to steal a march upon them with another coup which might be successful next time. However, the majority of the delegates felt the need of first confirming Wuelk's version of the Freie Pfalz movement. If Dr. Wuelk was right about the imminence of another attempt to seize power in the Palatinate, then Dorten should foreclose the issue by proclaiming his expansive concept of the Rhineland republic from Mainz or Wiesbaden before Haas and General Gérard could act. One of Dorten's co-workers, Dr. Franz Kingelschmitt of Mainz (who had been designated Minister of Fine Arts in the future cabinet), was sent to Spire to verify the reality of the plot.[57]

Klingelschmitt conferred with the Centrist leaders of the Palatinate. All of Dr. Wuelk's fears were quickly confirmed: a real *coup d'état* was being prepared at Spire, with the encouragement of General Gérard.[58] Klingelschmitt tried to obtain information from General Gérard, who told him, in effect, "to go to the devil with all his proclamations." [59] The would-be Minister of Fine Arts rushed by automobile back to Wiesbaden to tell Dorten that the adherents of the Freie Pfalz movement were going to act almost immediately by trying to seize the public buildings of Spire.[60] Dorten made haste to inform General Mangin of what was in store. Mangin had already corresponded with General Gérard about the current rumors, but the ardent republican and freemason general in Landau sent only vague and inconclusive answers to the questions of his conservative military colleague in Mainz.[61]

Klingelschmitt's fact-finding tour through the Palatinate had

[56] Dorten, *La tragédie rhénane*, p. 73.
[57] Dorten, *La tragédie rhénane*, p. 74.
[58] Dorten, *La tragédie rhénane*, p. 74.
[59] Guy de Traversay, p. 591.
[60] Dorten, *La tragédie rhénane*, p. 74.
[61] Dorten, *La tragédie rhénane*, p. 74.

precipitated events, for on the night of May 31, Dr. Wuelk telephoned Dorten that the Freie Pfalz committee was mobilizing its forces for a bid for power on June 1. Dorten consulted with the chiefs of his committees of the Rhineland, both of the North and South. They had already prepared a proclamation which had been approved by General Mangin on May 28. Mangin considered it "a great improvement over the first project." He took pride in having pointed out to Dorten's committee "the necessity in a first declaration, in the creation of a new state, of attributing to it diplomatic representation and control over questions of war, peace, and . . . commerce." [62]

Plans were approved by Mangin for issuing the proclamation, and for notifying the President of the Peace Conference of the new state through a petition sent through the channel of command reaching from the occupation commander to Marshal Foch.[63] The petition to be sent to the Versailles Conference read as follows:

The Premier designated by the Rhineland Committees to General Mangin, commander of French troops at Mayence:

The delegates of Rhenish Prussia, of Old Nassau, of Rhenish Hesse and of the Palatinate, in conformity with the urgent wishes expressed for the last six months by the Rhenish population, and after having deliberated at Aix-la-Chapelle, at Wiesbaden, at Mayence and at Spire, will proclaim on the date of June 1, 1919, the autonomy of the Rhineland Republic within the framework of Germany.

The new Republic will have for its capital Coblenz, the provisional seat of government being established at Wiesbaden.

In the hope of doing everything possible to bring about the conclusion of peace, and wishing to avoid all complications and all new deliberations, the delegates ask that the Peace Conference purely and simply recognize the existence of the new state whose popular constitution will be determined by statute.

Faithful to its fatherland so stricken by misfortune, but conscious of the terrible responsibility which Prussian militarism has imposed upon all of Germany, the new State has not sought in any devious way to evade

---

[62] General Charles Mangin, "Lettres de Rhénanie," p. 520.
[63] General Charles Mangin, "Lettres de Rhénanie," p. 520.

the burdens which are incumbent upon it in the reparation of damages caused in France and in Belgium.

The Rhineland population, seeking unfettered self-determination, is resolved to separate itself definitely from feudalism and Prussian militarism, so inimical to its memories and traditions.

It demands that the Allied and Associated Powers protect it, in the present and in the future, against the rancor and vengeance of those elements and those functionaries incapable of comprehending the justice and nobility of its aspirations, against all those who already threaten with imprisonment the supporters of Rhenish liberty. It depends upon [the Allied and Associated powers] for complete assurance of freedom in the approaching elections which will determine the status of the new Republic.[64]

Even before the posting of the Rhineland committees' proclamation, the Palatine conspirators of Dr. Haas were apprised of Dr. Dorten's intentions, and they in turn were determined not to be left behind. The intentions of the Freie Pfalz committee were an open secret, and the local Bavarian authorities in the Palatinate, realizing that they could not convince Munich that they had been caught by surprise, decided to resist Dr. Haas and his followers, come what may. The Social Democrats, powerful in the industrial city of Ludwigshafen, alerted their labor unionists to be ready to descend into the streets to resist Haas's coup. These dark omens had a discouraging effect upon most of the chemist's followers, despite the publicized fact of General Gérard's support of Palatine separatism. French soldiers could not be everywhere in the Palatinate, whereas anti-separatists could be—and indeed were. Abandoned by most of his followers, Dr. Haas, on June 1, nevertheless made his way into the Gambrinus Palace in Spire, the seat of the government. For a few minutes, Haas actually took possession of the office of the Bavarian governor, Herr Friedrich von Chlingensperg, the successor of the deported von Winterstein. But almost immediately thereafter a crowd of anti-separatists rushed into the building, preventing Haas from delivering his proclamation, and manhandling the biochemist and his small band of faithful follow-

---

[64] Dorten, *La tragédie rhénane*, p. 75.

ers. Only the quick arrival of General Gérard's French troops saved Haas from a fate worse than ridicule. General Gérard ordered the Palatinate press to remain silent on the Haas putsch. With delicate irony, Administrative President von Chlingensperg sent General Gérard his official thanks for the "benevolent attitude" and "the scrupulous reserve which the French military authority imposed upon itself when confronted with the political manifestations of June 1." [65]

No less comic was the outcome of Dr. Dorten's bid for power. In the early hours of June 1, 1919, after Klingelschmitt and Wuelk had warned him of the impending coup of the Freie Pfalz committee, Dorten ordered the proclamation of his Rhineland Republic posted in Spire, Wiesbaden, Mainz, and in several other towns of Hesse and Nassau. [66] This was all that time would allow. As soon as the posters were affixed, Dorten sent telegrams of notification to the Versailles Conference, to Friedrich Ebert, the President of the Reich, and to Chancellor Philipp Scheidemann. [67]

Dorten's posters met with as much curiosity as indignation on the part of the populace, since his seven cabinet members were no better known than Dorten himself. In several places the posting of the proclamation was resisted and the sheets were torn down. [68] There had been a complete change in cabinet membership since the American civil affairs officer, Colonel I. L. Hunt, had turned over Dorten's initial list to Chief Municipal Councilor Brandt for "investigation." Those who served with Dorten during his illusory tenure of office were Justice Minister Eckermann, a lawyer; Fine Arts

[65] Bavaria, Staatskommissar für die Pfalz. *Die Pfalz unter französischer Besetzung 1918–1924* (München, 1925), pp. 22–24; cf. article by Friedrich von Chlingensperg, "Ein Musterbeispiel französischer Gewaltpolitik," in *Dokumente aus dem Befreiungskampf der Pfalz,* Pfälzische Rundschau 1930, p. 10; see also Goebel, *Die pfälzische Presse,* pp. 91–92; also Oberhauser, *Kampf der Westmarck,* pp. 50–51, 55–56; also Jacquot, *General Gérard und die Pfalz,* p. 122; also Gedye, *The Revolver Republic,* p. 43.

[66] *Kölnische Zeitung,* June 3, 1919; *Frankfurter Zeitung,* June 2, 1919.
[67] *Die Gruende,* pp. 46–47.
[68] Allen, *The Rhineland Occupation,* pp. 194–195.

Minister Klingelschmitt, a teacher; Education Minister Kremer, a teacher; General Welfare Minister Kraemer, a labor unionist; Finance minister Dr. Liebling; Interior Minister Monikes; and Agriculture Minister Salm.[69] Nonentities though they were, Dorten's cabinet members solemnly accompanied their intrepid leader through the streets of Wiesbaden to the Landeshaus of Nassau to take symbolic possession of the seat of provincial government and to await developments—especially the anticipated word from the Peace Conference.

No answer reached them from Versailles, but there were immediate repercussions from Cologne and Mainz, where the Social Democrats organized demonstrations hostile to separatism.[70] The German mayor of Mainz requested an audience with General Mangin to learn whom he should obey henceforth, Dr. Dorten or Herr Scheidemann.[71] The following day the mayor of Wiesbaden, Herr Meister, was ordered to appear at French headquarters where he was bluntly told by the commandant of the city to obey the orders of Dorten's provisional government. When Herr Meister protested that as a Prussian official he could not recognize the authority of Dorten's band, and consequently wished to be relieved of his office, the French commandant complied at once, replacing him with Herr Springorum, an assistant of the mayor.[72]

On the night of June 2 the French military authorities sent over their telegraph lines the following dispatch:

Mayence No. 11523B. This morning Rhine Republic was proclaimed in all cities without difficulty. Provisional government presided over by Doctor Dorten is at present installed at Wiesbaden and is obeyed. This event, which ends annoying uncertainty, appears desirable to majority of population. Doctor Dorten has addressed message to Marshal Foch,

[69] American Military Government of Occupied Germany, 1918–1920, I, 394, in the Henry T. Allen Papers.

[70] American Military Government of Occupied Germany, 1918–1920, I, 395, in the Henry T. Allen Papers; cf. Brüggemann, *Die Rheinische Republik*, p. 109.

[71] Dorten, *La tragédie rhénane*, p. 79.

[72] Allen, *The Rhineland Occupation*, p. 195.

to the Conference, and to all generals commanding armies of occupation for their respective governments.[73]

In this telegram the French military wish sired the thought of the popularity of Dorten's Republic. Reality was quite otherwise. In Western Germany there were widespread strikes in protest and numerous expressions of opposition.[74] On June 2 the Rhenish deputies of the German National Assembly and of the Prussian Assembly, except for several Centrists, drew up a formal repudiation of Dorten's Rhineland republic.[75] The infant state was clearly not viable.

The *coup de grâce* was administered by none other than Clemenceau, acting first through correspondence, and also through his Under-Secretary of State.[76] Jules Jeanneney arrived from Paris on June 3, simultaneously with Mangin's receipt of a letter from Clemenceau. In this letter Clemenceau summarized for Mangin the account which Jeanneney had given of his fact-finding trip in the Rhineland to learn what the French generals were doing in promoting separatism. Mangin was reminded that he had sent emissaries to General Liggett, General Robertson, and General Michel to win their indulgence toward the separatists. Clemenceau acknowledged that Mangin had reported to his chiefs, but "without having consulted them." He conceded that it was proper for Mangin to have given intelligence data on the Rhenish republic plot to his Allied military colleagues. But what was not permissible was for him to advise his colleagues "as to the political attitude which it was proper for them to take." Political questions appertained to the government, not to the military command. A French commander had no authority "to pronounce . . . in advance on the merit of a new political constitution for a country which he controls." He had even less justification for proclaiming his views on the political future of a sector held by an Allied country. Clemenceau concluded his

[73] Allen, p. 195.

[74] American Military Government of Occupied Germany, 1918–1920, I, 395, in the Henry T. Allen Papers; see also *Kölnische Zeitung,* June 2, 1919.

[75] *Kölnische Volkszeitung,* June 3, 1919; cf. Allen, p. 195.

[76] Dorten, *La tragédie rhénane,* p. 79.

letter with one of his characteristically mild reproofs to his generals: "I must . . . recall you to strict observ[ance] of complete neutrality in everything which has to do with purely political affairs in the occupied countries. I ask you, at the same time, to refrain from all interference with the Allied generals, [apart from] such cases as are provided for by military regulations." [77]

Reinforcing the tenor of this letter was Clemenceau's oral instruction to Mangin, which was transmitted by Jules Jeanneney. Clemenceau's "inspector general" had traveled to Mainz by way of Kaiserslautern, where he had seen a mob so excited over the separatist proclamation that force had to be used to disperse it. He had gone on through Landau, where a Prussian had been killed in an affray between anti-separatists and separatists. Using these ugly incidents as a text, Jeanneney delivered a "homily" to Mangin and to his superior officer General Fayolle.[78] The generals were told, politely, to have nothing further to do with the separatists.[79] They had no choice but to capitulate to Clemenceau, although Mangin, sensitive to a point of honor, naturally felt obliged to protect such separatist leaders as Dorten from the wrath of their fellow countrymen.[80]

Dorten was soon to need such protection. After he and his "cabinet" had installed themselves in the Landeshaus at Wiesbaden, the seat of the provincial government of Nassau, he was prompted to demonstrate his new authority. All he could think of was to dictate to several stenographers a scheme for the restoration of the University of Mainz.[81] It had been impossible for him to see General Mangin (who was at Mainz) either on June 1 or June 2, but early on the morning of June 2 Dorten was visited by Colonel Pinot, the French superior administrator of the district of Wiesbaden,[82] who had told him earlier that "the French Republic would

[77] Baker, *Woodrow Wilson and World Settlement,* II, 85–92.

[78] General Charles Mangin, "Lettres de Rhénanie," p. 524.

[79] Dorten, *La tragédie rhénane,* pp. 79, 81; cf. Major Louis Mangin, *La France et le Rhin,* p. 57.

[80] Dorten, *La tragédie rhénane,* p. 79.

[81] Guy de Traversay, "La première tentative de République rhénane," p. 591.

[82] American Military Government of Occupied Germany, 1918–1920, I, 400, in the Henry T. Allen Papers.

not allow the creation of a priestly state on the Rhine." The colonel appeared completely changed now, for he strongly encouraged Dorten to seize the Prussian governmental palace of the Administrative President in Wiesbaden, which would be a conquest in addition to the provincial Landeshaus of Nassau which he and his cabinet already occupied. The colonel gave Dorten a revolver to enable him to force an entrance into the palace, which would be easy since the Prussians in the building were unarmed. The colonel told Dorten that this advice was upon General Mangin's express instructions—a monstrous falsehood, as Dorten later discovered. A sympathetic French captain whispered to Dorten that it would be better to entrust the revolver to him, and "to be on his guard against everything." [83]

Although forewarned, Dorten and his "cabinet" nevertheless left the Landeshaus for the Prussian governmental palace, where their entry was unopposed, with even a Prussian police commissioner yielding to them. Dorten and his band walked through the building in a vain search for the Prussian prefect. The separatists then took possession of the prefect's office.

Suddenly the office door was flung open and the prefect and a score of Prussian functionaries burst into the room. When Dorten raised his hand to silence the clamor the prefect cried out, "He's going to shoot!" and bolted from the room, followed by his functionaries.[84] A few minutes later a band of "hooligans" forced an entrance into the office, and they used sticks and knives upon the "government" of the Rhineland republic, injuring Herr Eckermann and Herr Kremer.[85] There was pandemonium among the clerks and stenographers, who hid under the tables.[86]

The farce was abruptly ended when the superior administrator of Wiesbaden, Colonel Pinot (who, as an adversary of Mangin's, and as a proponent of annexation, had apparently wanted to give separatist Dorten sufficient rope for hanging himself) strode into

[83] Dorten, *La tragédie rhénane,* p. 80.

[84] Dorten, *La tragédie rhénane,* p. 80.

[85] American Military Government of Occupied Germany, 1918–1820, I, 400, in the Henry T. Allen Papers.

[86] Guy de Traversay, "La première tentative de République rhénane," p. 591.

the room, flicking his riding crop against his boots, and exclaiming: "Let's go! It's finished!" [87] It was not altogether finished, for on the following day Dorten tried another seizure of power in Birkenfeld, but with even less success than in Wiesbaden.[88] The Rhineland republic was beyond doubt stillborn.

The outside world reacted quickly to the news of Dorten's *coup d'état*. President Poincaré was one of the first Frenchmen to welcome the word of the republic's proclamation on June 1. Immediately after receiving a telegram from General Mangin informing him of the anxiously hoped-for event, the President of the French Republic sent a message to Clemenceau, in which he made the following revealing comment:

> I suppose that the general would not have transmitted this . . . to me if the movement was not a serious one, and if it is serious I hope that the Allies will not compel us to suppress it.
>
> Since the Rhineland Republic is forming itself "within the system of the German Empire," it is not even an act of separatism, and as a popular vote, on the other hand, is promised, there seems to be nothing that might shock President Wilson.
>
> In my opinion it would be very unfortunate if we were to take part against these as yet very shy dispositions towards independence.[89]

This message from Poincaré irritated Clemenceau, who was disgusted with the entire question of Rhineland separatism, so clearly a forlorn hope. In his apologia Clemenceau had the following to say about Poincaré's part in the fiasco:

> I invite the reader to appreciate this "supposition" of M. Poincaré's, intended to divert from him any suspicion of an understanding with General Mangin. The President of the Republic is a partisan (discreet but determined) of the seizure by the French of the Rhineland, annexation childishly referred to under the subterfuge of another name. He has spoken of it with General Mangin . . . and General Mangin takes it into his head, in his turn, to go beyond my instructions. So he negotiates

---

[87] Dorten, *La tragédie rhénane,* p. 81; cf. American Military Government of Occupied Germany, 1918–1920, I, 400, in the Henry T. Allen Papers.

[88] Guy de Traversay, p. 591.

[89] Quoted in Clemenceau, *Grandeur and Misery,* pp. 223–224.

with Dorten . . . and he goes so far as to undertake to negotiate with the military chiefs of the Allies apart from their Governments, while he himself applies to the President of the Republic, who is not entitled to solve this question, or any other, without the Ministers he has chosen.

If he had done his duty, M. Poincaré would have returned his document to the insubordinate general, asking him to communicate the text, in the first place, to the Minister of War.[90]

In regard to this point, Clemenceau's caustic critic, Georges Vial-Mazel, contended that, since "General Mangin had never received a reply in response to his letters and reports" sent to the Minister of War, it was not appropriate for Clemenceau to reproach the general for negligence.[91] But the Tiger was not reproaching Mangin for negligence, since he conceded that Mangin had "informed his chiefs" (although Clemenceau denied knowledge of the general's talks with Dorten), but rather he accused him of violating the hierarchical order in by-passing the Prime Minister and Minister of War by communicating directly with the President of the Republic, who had no legal responsibility in the matter, but who was known to be a partisan of Rhenish separatism. Clemenceau was under no legal obligation to correspond with the French commanders of the army of occupation, whereas Mangin was obligated to report to his chiefs. It would have been courtly of Clemenceau to have replied to Mangin, but while it would have been a wise move for Clemenceau to have explained his government's Rhineland policy to Foch and Poincaré, he was under no obligation to spell out its refinements to the field commanders.

The inevitable foreign criticism of French subornation of separatism came not from President Wilson or Lloyd George, but from the German peace delegation at Versailles. Count Brockdorff-Rantzau, the Foreign Minister and chief of the delegation, sent Clemenceau, as President of the Peace Conference, a strong protest. Brockdorff-Rantzau stated that the German delegation had learned from the press, as well as from direct reports from Germany, of

[90] Clemenceau, p. 223.

[91] Vial-Mazel, *Erreurs et oublis de Georges Clemenceau,* p. 110.

the separatist efforts in the Rhineland and the Palatinate. He charged that the plots to create autonomous republics were not only tolerated by the French military authorities but openly abetted. When German administrators performed their duty by taking action against the traitorous conspirators, these loyal officials were threatened with prosecution and expulsion by the French occupation authorities. The sealing off of the Rhine districts from the rest of Germany did not permit on-the-spot verification of the reports of the conspiracies, but the gravamina were contained in a note (a copy of which was enclosed) from the German member of the armistice commission, Matthias Erzberger, to General Nudant, the French President of the Interallied Armistice Commission.

The German delegation, continued Brockdorff-Rantzau, wanted to call the attention of the Allied governments to the fact that any encouragement of efforts to detach the Western territories from Germany would have a disturbing effect upon the peace negotiations, and prejudice the execution of such a treaty as might be concluded. Connivance at separatism would contravene Article V, Paragraph 2 of the armistice agreement, which expressly recognized the continuing authority of German administrators in the occupied territories, as well as the inviolable union of those territories with the Empire.

Brockdorff-Rantzau concluded this protest with the reminder that Germany would be in a position to make reparation payments only if its productive capacity remained unimpaired. The severance of the densely populated, industrialized regions of the Rhineland would obviously hamper Germany's ability to offer guarantees for the execution of the conditions of the peace. Therefore, the German peace delegation urgently requested the Allied and Associated governments to make clear to the occupation authorities the danger of their mistaken political zeal. They should be forbidden from encouraging defection on the part of German citizens, nor should they be allowed to prevent the German authorities from dutifully opposing separatist efforts.[92]

[92] Woodrow Wilson Papers.

The enclosure referred to in Brockdorff-Rantzau's letter was a note, dated June 2, 1919, which the German civilian member of the armistice commission, Minister without portfolio Matthias Erzberger, had addressed to the chief French armistice commissioner at Spa, General Nudant. Erzberger wrote that the German government had received word that the French occupation authorities in the districts on the Left bank of the Rhine had encouraged and abetted "treasonable practices" in the occupied territories, in violation of the armistice. The German government regretted that it was not in a position to investigate on the spot the accuracy of these reports. The information received was to the effect that unauthorized persons who were "devoid of any political influence" had been making repeated efforts to proclaim a Rhenish republic which would be severed from the German Empire. These conspirators had consulted General Mangin, General Gérard, Colonel Pinot, and Captain Rostan, the French censor in Aachen.

Erzberger asserted that the French occupation authorities had allowed the posting of the proclamation of a Rhenish republic on June 1, while other occupation authorities had prohibited the publication of Chancellor Scheidemann's warning of May 29 that separatist efforts would be prosecuted as high treason. When the anonymous proclamation of a Rhenish republic was posted in Mainz on June 1 and indignant residents of the city had responded by tearing down most of the posters, the French military authorities had ordered the arrest and detention of those loyal Germans who had removed the *affiches*. When a group of patriotic Germans had gone to see Colonel Pinot to protest against the condoning of separatism, the French military administrator had threatened a German official who was a member of the delegation with a blockade of food shipments to such towns as would not accept the new republic.

It was charged further by Erzberger that Administrative President von Winterstein had been expelled from the Palatinate because of his opposition to separatist efforts there. Moreover, the French military authorities had readily accepted telegrams addressed to the Peace Conference in Paris and to President Ebert and Chancellor Scheidemann, by "a public prosecutor, one Dorten of Wiesbaden, who on his own authority [had] arrogated to himself the title of President of the new republic." This nonentity had addressed to the Peace Conference a request "to be allowed to travel to Paris for the purpose of negotiations."

Erzberger concluded his note with the assertion that "these acts of French authorities of the occupying armies are utterly at variance with the conditions of the armistice . . . and the declaration of Marshal Foch. . . . The German government enters the most decided protest against this conduct and confidently expects the authorities of the occupying armies to forbear, particularly during the peace negotiations, from doing anything . . . conducive to disturbing, and even rendering impossible, successful progress in the negotiations for peace." [93]

These protests indicated that the would-be diplomats, Foch, Mangin, and Gérard, had played directly into the hands of the Germans and the British. Berlin could now argue plausibly that since the French were virtually scrapping the Treaty of Versailles by promoting a transparently disguised annexation of the Rhineland, the Germans could reconsider the whole question of signing the treaty. British Prime Minister Lloyd George could regard the Palatine-Rhenish rebellion as a made-to-order pretext for trying to obtain guarantees of French withdrawal from Germany, not at the end of fifteen years as set forth in the treaty draft, but at the end of a scant one or two year occupation. [94] The British had all along been determined to preclude French domination of the Rhineland which would confer a great military advantage upon France, not to mention the boon to French metallurgy which would become dangerously competitive with the British. Lloyd George could now contend that so long as French forces were in the Rhineland, they would ceaselessly foment coups and rebellions to try to bring about a disguised annexation, as Mangin and Gérard had just attempted with Foch's blessing. [95] This would be a constant source of friction

[93] Woodrow Wilson Papers.

[94] Tardieu, *The Truth About the Treaty*, p. 372.

[95] Lloyd George, *The Truth*, I, 581–582; cf. Clemenceau, *Grandeur and Misery*, p. 218.

among France, its Allies, and Germany, thereby endangering the peace to a greater extent than a completely unoccupied Germany, in Lloyd George's view.

Lloyd George seized the occasion afforded by Dorten's *putsch* to wage, in the inner counsels of the Big Four, a hard battle against a prolonged occupation of Germany. His campaign lasted for two weeks, and it taxed Clemenceau's powers to the utmost to retrieve the French diplomatic position in regard to the treaty.[96] After some stormy scenes with Lloyd George, Clemenceau at last agreed to a compromise formula: "If, before the expiration of the period of fifteen years, Germany has satisfied all the obligations resulting for it from the present treaty, the occupation troops will be immediately withdrawn." [97] This compromise salvaged the French position, since the contingency would hardly arise in which Germany would pay off all its reparations in less than fifteen years. Moreover, France still possessed the right of reoccupying the Rhineland in the future in case of German violation of the treaty.

Clemenceau would have been more than justified in summarily dismissing Mangin and Gérard for undercutting his handling of France's foreign policy, yet he acted with his accustomed judiciousness in disciplining the generals. Apart from his letter of mild remonstrance to Mangin, and his sending of Jules Jeanneney on his "inspector general's" mission to Landau and Mainz, he bided his time for four months before final correction. The Tiger's reasons for slowness and moderation were obvious. Clemenceau's political enemies in Parliament would try to capitalize upon the generals' dismissal, using it as an excuse for striking back at the Tiger because of his enforced concessions to Lloyd George and Wilson on the Rhineland. This would be a preliminary skirmish before repudiating the entire treaty and driving Clemenceau from political life in the forthcoming general elections scheduled for November 1919.[98] Although Clemenceau naturally wanted to avoid his own

[96] Clemenceau, p. 218; cf. Mordacq, *Le ministère Clemenceau,* III, 299; cf. Tardieu, p. 372; see also Gedye, *The Revolver Republic,* pp. 47–48.

[97] Mordacq, III, 316–317.

[98] Tardieu, *The Truth About the Treaty,* p. 216.

political demise, this seems to have been a lesser consideration with the aged statesman. Furthermore, he was not looking for convenient scapegoats for Marshal Foch who was ultimately responsible for the occupation commanders' suborning the separatists. Clemenceau spelled out Foch's role in this affair at a meeting of the Big Three on June 16, 1919. As the Tiger acknowledged to Wilson and Lloyd George: "The marshal has placed at Mainz and Köln [actually at Landau] two generals of whom one, Mangin, is a good soldier but a bad politician, while the other, Gérard, is a mediocre soldier and an execrable politician. He has placed them there with political intent. A policy of separatism is what he offers us." [99] The Tiger waited for the acceptance of the Treaty of Versailles by Parliament, and then in October 1919 he reorganized the French armies of occupation by abolishing the army group of General Fayolle, which had comprised the Tenth Army of Mangin and the Eighth Army of Gérard. All three generals were relieved of their commands and were replaced by a single commander of the permanent French Army of the Rhine, General Degoutte.[100] Once again Clemenceau demonstrated not only political cunning but a high order of statesmanship.

Marshal Foch terminated his indefatigable campaign against the treaty with one final gesture of obstruction—this time of an overt nature, and not in the form of egging on his subordinates. The Germans had been given a convenient pretext for refusing to sign the treaty by the revelation of French annexationist skulduggery in the Haas and Dorten affairs. Small wonder, then, that the German government—especially Chancellor Scheidemann and Foreign Minister Brockdorff-Rantzau—tried to exploit to the utmost the diplomatic advantage conferred upon them by the maladroit French generals. The victorious Allies became so restive over the German delay in signing the treaty that they decided on June 16, 1919, to submit an ultimatum to Germany: either sign the peace within five days, or the armistice would be automatically terminated and hostilities resumed. Marshal Foch—who had begun to appear com-

[99] Mantoux, ed., *Les délibérations du conseil des quatre,* II, 444.
[100] Henry T. Allen Papers.

pletely incorrigible to Clemenceau, Lloyd George, and Wilson— found in this latest impasse still another opportunity for trying to divide Germany.

That Foch's determination was as strong as ever came out when he was questioned by Wilson, Lloyd George, and Clemenceau on June 16 as to the readiness of his Allied forces to resume military operations. The Big Three were astounded by the marshal's devious reply, which suggested that he had learned little and forgotten less during the past eight months. For the first time, and at the thirteenth hour, Foch pleaded poverty of the forces which would be needed to carry out a march upon Berlin.[101] He said that he commanded only thirty-nine Allied divisions, whereas on November 11, 1918, he had ninety under his command. It could be foreseen that German military resistance would not be massive against his thirty-nine divisions, but it was to be remembered that the German population of sixty-five million had in its midst many demobilized officers and soldiers capable of offering serious guerrilla resistance on the flanks and in the rear of a direct Allied march of the four hundred and eighty kilometres necessary to reach Berlin from the Rhine. But if the Allies decided upon detaching South Germany from the North, while marching up the Main valley, they would be confronted by only forty-five million Germans.

Foch stated as follows the gist of his hastily improvised scheme: "A strategy of separation, aided by a policy of separation, would allow us to reach the head of the German organism, Berlin. The question is this—are we willing to treat with the separate states, Baden, Württemberg, Bavaria?"[102] Foch slightly amplified his new proposal: "To march upon Berlin with 39 divisions, some of which would have to protect communications, would bring us [there] in a weakened condition and threatened on our right flank. We could avoid this by putting South Germany out of action through special treatment and a definitive peace."[103] Woodrow Wilson wanted a clarification of this novel scheme. But Foch had already given out

[101] Baker, *Woodrow Wilson and World Settlement*, II, 99.
[102] Mantoux, ed., *Les délibérations du conseil des quatre*, II, 432.
[103] Mantoux, II, 432.

as much of his intention as he cared to reveal. He repeated, "The States of the South are the first we would meet on our march, and we would treat with them." [104] Lloyd George wanted to know what would be the share of reparations incumbent upon the South German states to be thus dismembered. Again Foch replied deviously, "I would impose upon them an immediate accounting; then they could calculate their share of the contribution." [105] Lloyd George expressed the objection that, by so doing, the Allies would deprive themselves of the full reparation which could be recovered from an integrated Germany, or else if the dismembered states were treated the same as the rest of Germany, there would be no inducement for them "to come over to us."

It was obvious that the discussion was straying from Marshal Foch's province. "It is not necessary to mix policy with strategy," Clemenceau said. "For policy is outside [Marshal Foch's] role. Policy does not mix in military estimates any more than strategy intervenes in our counsels here. If Marshal Foch foresees difficulties, he is right to make them known to us. But we must see the other side of the picture. Germany has 65 million inhabitants, but it is defeated, and German reaction to defeat is different from the French. In Germany there are many men who have been good soldiers, but they are beaten, and Germans resist only if they are organized." [106]

The session adjourned and after a few hours reassembled, this time with Marshal Foch absent and with Italian Foreign Minister Sonnino's presence making it a Big Four session. President Wilson broached the subject of Foch's latest stratagem: "I do not know what to think of what Marshal Foch has just said to us. I cannnot imagine what has happened since we last heard him." Lloyd George remarked that "Marshal Foch appears to me to be dominated by purely political considerations. He wants to return to a policy of the past, to a time when France aimed at the conquest of the Left

---

[104] Mantoux, II, 433.

[105] Mantoux, II, 433; cf. Baker, *Woodrow Wilson and World Settlement*, II, 99.

[106] Mantoux, II, 433.

bank of the Rhine. . . . I fear that the influence of General Wey-gand [Marshal Foch's Chief of Staff] is not for the good. I see him speaking ceaselessly into the ear of the marshal and suggesting to him what to say." President Wilson expressed the belief that Foch "has seen his schemes founder, and he does not want to assist in the execution of ours." [107]

Prime Minister Clemenceau felt obligated to say something about Foch's latest maneuver without completely repudiating the marshal. "When we have questioned Marshal Foch about his military plans," said Clemenceau, "he has replied to us: 'Formulate a policy of separatism!' What does one say to that . . . ? I keenly regret the attitude taken by Marshal Foch. I believe, as you do, in the influence of General Weygand, but I must say in his favor that he is a staff officer of the first order." [108]

President Wilson and Lloyd George expressed misgivings over entrusting military operations to so obstinate and intractable a figure as Marshal Foch, who had revealed a conception of policy entirely at variance with that of the heads of state.[109] Clemenceau recalled that Foch had never complained before of an insufficiency of forces at his disposal.[110]

The next day, on June 17, the Big Four took up a note which they had just received from Marshal Foch. In it Marshal Foch had adroitly substituted the idea of "separate armistices" for Baden, Württemberg, and Bavaria in place of "separate peace treaties," thereby strengthening his legitimate role as a strategist rather than a policy-maker. President Wilson expressed the view that "this note leaves us where we were." [111] Clemenceau proposed to write "a letter in which we say that we do not understand what [Foch] has written on the subject of the armistices to be concluded; for the armistice is not our affair but his. I will not say a word about a

[107] Mantoux, II, 442.

[108] Mantoux, II, 443.

[109] Mantoux, II, 444.

[110] Mantoux, II, 443; cf. Baker, *Woodrow Wilson and World Settlement,* II, 99.

[111] Mantoux, II, 447; cf. Baker, II, 99.

policy of separatism: it is best to let that go." Lloyd George expressed an understandable irritation with the marshal: "It seems [Foch] always has something in his head. . . . We must be on guard. He is an obstinate man, and I am afraid that instead of going straight to Berlin, he will follow a policy of the dislocation of the German Empire which would cause infinite difficulties for us. I would much rather see there a man like Pétain, but I do not propose replacing Marshal Foch." [112]

Clemenceau had reason to be grateful for the understanding and sympathy of his civilian colleagues who understood Foch's presumption, stubbornness, patriotism, and political "nuisance value" quite as well as the French Prime Minister. With his vast international prestige, Foch was admittedly hard to handle—a formidable figure. As for the removal of Foch, Clemenceau commented: "After the letter which he has just written us we cannot do that. We can hold him under surveillance, and we can judge his acts. At present he has all the glamor of victory." [113]

Three days later, on June 20, Marshal Foch appeared again in person before the Big Four to repeat his proposal of marching circuitously toward Berlin via Prague and Posen, thereby linking up with the Czechs and the Poles for the purpose of closing a ring around Berlin. Along the route of march separate armistices would be arranged with the South German states.[114] Foch made surprising headway at this session of the Big Four by almost winning over to his scheme British Foreign Secretary Arthur Balfour. The British Foreign Secretary was apparently impressed with the concurrence of the Allied generals in Foch's plan of the indirect march via Prague and Posen. "A [direct] march upon Berlin presents too many risks for it to be undertaken," Balfour said.

Our first effort should aim at putting South Germany out of action. I think that desirable. I acknowledge some doubts as to the possibility of achieving it. Marshal Foch has not told us upon what he bases his hope of having the states of South Germany sign separate armistices. To go

[112] Mantoux, II, 448.
[113] Mantoux, II, 448.
[114] Mantoux, II, 464.

from there to the Weser we must either detach South Germany or re-inforce our armies. . . . We must avoid anything which could give the appearance of a check. But this is purely a political question . . . a question of opinion.[115]

Balfour wondered about the feasibility of the separate armistices, as desirable as they might be in the abstract. He put the direct question to the Big Four: "Suppose Württemberg demands an armistice and you reply: 'Come sign the peace with the Allies.' With whom will you sign it? Could the treaty which we have prepared be thus cut into pieces for the different states of Germany?" [116] Clemenceau replied that he fully understood Balfour's doubts: "It is certain that it would be necessary to remake the whole treaty. That is why I would confine myself to the response: 'Come to Versailles and we shall make peace with you.'" [117] This was a vague enough recommendation to satisfy almost anyone— except the Germans, including the Württembergers, all of whom had a high threshold of suspicion. The Big Four decided to wait until receiving the final word from the Germans as to whether they would sign the treaty. Then they could formulate the new policy.[118]

Foch was perhaps on the verge of a great triumph—possibly his greatest achievement during his prolonged campaign against the Treaty of Versailles. It appeared that he was actually keeping open the door for further maneuvers which might conceivably have dismembered Germany. This is conjecture, for there was no further opportunity to put the strategem to the test. The strength of German nationalism was such that, in all likelihood, no component state would have actually agreed to a separate armistice or a separate peace, since the danger of atomizing the German Reich was self-evident to all Germans. There was at the time in Germany a fever of nationalism manifesting itself in patriotic protests against the "Diktat" of Versailles, the stern provisions of which had become

[115] Mantoux, II, 464–465.
[116] Mantoux, II, 466.
[117] Mantoux, II, 466.
[118] Baker, *Woodrow Wilson and World Settlement,* II, 99.

well known. Had there been a march upon Berlin—especially by Foch's circuitous route—the diplomatic prospects would have been prejudiced, especially if separate armistices had been actually offered the South German states—and rejected, as they undoubtedly would have been. But the Germans themselves closed the door upon Foch's hopes by sending word on June 22, 1919, that since Scheidemann and Brockdorff-Rantzau had resigned rather than sign the Treaty of Versailles, a new government was being formed which would sign, albeit under protest.[119] This capitulation dissipated realistic prospect of a dismembered Germany just as it seemed feasible. All of Foch's tireless efforts, his reiterated demands and protests, his bristling defiance, his threat of resignation, his "leaks" to the press, his devious maneuvers, appeared to be in vain. As a silent protest, Foch absented himself from the ceremony in the Hall of Mirrors at Versailles on June 28, when the treaty was signed by the German plenipotentiaries.[120] Foch acknowledged, "On that day I took refuge in my headquarters at Kreuznach." [121]

[119] Baker, II, 99–100.
[120] George Aston, *Marshal Foch* (New York, 1929), p. 426.
[121] Quoted in Liddell Hart, *Foch,* p. 427.

Chapter V

Clemenceau's Peace

Even after Germany's signing of the treaty, Marshal Foch, as a theoretical possibility, could still have been vindicated by the French Parliament. It was conceivable—if unlikely—that the deputies might refuse to ratify the treaty. Many parliamentarians supported Foch's views on the Rhineland question, and the marshal must have had mixed feelings as the ratification debates brought opposition to Clemenceau's compromise peace into the open at last. Parliament had maintained a moody silence on the Rhineland question until two months after the treaty was signed. Then, on August 26, 1919, the parliamentarians began what proved to be nearly six weeks of prolix but ineffectual debate on the treaty, with most of the pronouncements obviously made "for the political record." It was apparent to almost everyone that France would eventually have to acquiesce in the compromise peace, for all its shortcomings, unless the nation wished to be left alone on the continent with a vengeful Germany.

An indication of the widespread support of Foch's position on the Rhineland may be found in the fact that even a Socialist Deputy in good standing, Francois Fournier, criticized the treaty because it did not provide for "the return to France of the Left bank of the Rhine, which geographically belongs to it." [1] A Socialist militant, Albert Thomas, found himself aligned with rightist Deputy Maurice Barrès in demanding the military occupation of the Rhineland. He acknowledged that the French government had given valid reasons for such a military occupation in its memorandum of

[1] *Annales de la Chambre* . . . Séance du 26 aout 1919, p. 3617.

February 25, 1919, reasons which were repeated in Clemenceau's note of March 17.[2]

But these views of Fournier and Thomas were not at all characteristic of the Socialists. In fact, Thomas soon reverted to the main Socialist thesis with his statement: "Instead of trying to alienate Germany, we ought to be trying to support those German elements with whom an entente is possible; we ought to support the democratic Germany, to reach an accord with those Germans who themselves recognize the guilt of their country." [3] Typical of the Socialist position on the treaty was the statement of Deputy Fréderic Brunet: "To protect our territory, the military leaders demanded a frontier [the Rhine] which violated the conscience of peoples. The government preferred a treaty guaranteed by America and England, for which I congratulate them. But the moral and material guarantees of the future will be found in the League of Nations." [4] For all the Socialists' approval of Clemenceau's correctness in abandoning the demands for the Rhine frontier, two-thirds of them nevertheless voted against the treaty and a third abstained at the close of the long debate, chiefly because the treaty failed to reduce sufficiently the role of the German military, thereby weakening the position of the German Social Democrats.

Some Radicals were more favorably disposed than the Socialists toward Clemenceau's compromise peace. Radical Deputy René Renoult, the President of the Army Commission, told his colleagues of the Chamber that they should be at ease about the question of the Rhine frontier which disturbed so many of the speakers, for France should not be made to appear bent upon conquest. He felt that the great merit of the treaty was that it demonstrated France's peaceful intentions. A well-organized defensive frontier behind which armament could be safely reduced would provide sufficient protection.[5] Marshal Foch found a critic in Radical Deputy Margaine—and a technical critic, at that. Margaine attacked the Mar-

[2] *Annales,* 29 aout 1919, p. 3662.
[3] *Annales,* 29 aout 1919, p. 3665.
[4] *Annales,* 28 aout 1919, p. 3647.
[5] E. Beau de Loménie, *Le débat de ratification du traité de Versailles* (Paris, 1945), p. 214.

shal's Rhineland scheme on the novel strategic grounds that it was infeasible to try to defend France by making a stand along a river course such as the Rhine. Deputy Margaine declared: "I see our general staff today . . . waging a sort of quiet campaign . . . circulating documents . . . about the mistake of not acquiring the Rhine as the frontier. . . . When, as a layman, I consider the war, it seems to me that the impassable barriers are not rivers or streams . . . but massive forests." [6] Margaine, unfortunately, did not elaborate upon precisely which "massive forests" should constitute France's impenetrable frontier.

Marshal Foch was supported by Radical Deputy Franklin-Bouillon, who took to task peace conference delegate André Tardieu for trying to justify the abandonment of the Rhineland by citing all the objections of the Allies. Addressing Tardieu directly, Frankin-Bouillon said, "You always appear to be pleading extenuating circumstances as regards the Allies, and to be critical of Marshal Foch." Then he repeated the argument of Barrès that in demanding an independent Rhenish state, "it is not the unity of Germany which we are trying to destroy, but the hegemony of Prussia." [7]

The moderate parliamentary view of the treaty was perhaps best expressed by Charles Benoist, the chief *rapporteur* of the Treaty Commission, a historian and a member of the Institute. "France could have in the East," he said, "only one good military frontier, the Rhine. Never have we had peace or security when the Rhine was not this frontier. . . . No foreign guarantee can by itself take the place of this safeguard." Benoist quoted Heinrich Heine to the effect that the "Rhinelanders were neither German nor French but Belgian." Benoist contended that the French had not "demanded the Left bank of the Rhine for ourselves, but for the Rhinelanders," who would be consulted in conformity with the principles of self-determination.[8] In similar vein, the moderate Deputy de Chappedelaine said: "After the armistice of November 11, France expected the Peace Conference to draw its military frontier at the Rhine.

[6] *Annales,* 30 septembre 1919, p. 4204.
[7] *Annales,* 27 aout 1919, p. 3633.
[8] *Annales,* 3 septembre 1919, p. 3711.

The history and interests of our country demand it. . . . But in observance of the principle of self-determination of peoples, and rejecting any idea of having in the French Parliament a single deputy under protest, the Conference excluded any idea of conquest or annexation, even of territories which belonged to us until not long ago. The nation had not expected the annexation of the Left bank of the Rhine, but rather the drawing of its military frontier at the Rhine." Deputy de Chappedelaine reproved the Clemenceau government for its mistake of "always having referred to the river as the Western limit of Germany" without making it sufficiently clear that only France's military frontier—*not* its political frontier—would be on the Rhine.[9]

Another moderate Deputy, Raiberti, expressed regret that France was recovering its frontier of 1870 instead of that of 1814. "But as a whole, France can approve the treaty, reflecting as it does [French] ideas and . . . historical traditions. France has been the first among the states to proclaim the right of self-determination. . . . France renounces once again all spirit of conquest. . . . It demands only the restoration of ancient frontiers. Everyone knows that not for an instant during the peace negotiations did it raise demands for the possession of the Left bank of the Rhine. By this tacit renunciation, it has . . . contributed to proclaiming . . . the birth of a new right in the realm of liberty and justice." [10] A final example of the moderate position was the statement of Deputy Cornudet:

Never have I heard anyone say that France contemplated annexation, imperialism or conquest. . . . What do we all demand? That future generations be spared the horrors of war; that our national defense be assured. . . . The military frontier of the Rhine was not simply the plan of our general staff, for had it been, the government could not have adopted the idea with any authority or conviction. What must one conclude? That there was resistance. . . . But we have never demanded annexation of the Left bank of the Rhine. We demand simply that the inhabitants of these territories be organized according to their own wishes, removed from Prussian sovereignty, which is of recent origin.[11]

[9] *Annales,* 27 aout 1919, pp. 3638–3639.
[10] *Annales,* 26 aout 1919, pp. 3606–3607.
[11] *Annales,* 26 aout 1919, pp. 3612–3614.

The viewpoint of the royalist Right was expressed by the Catholic Deputy de Gailhard-Bancel, who attacked the peacemakers for anti-Catholic bias, especially as regards the Hapsburg Empire. De Gailhard-Bancel contended that the peacemakers were correct in compelling Austro-Hungary to cede all the border areas demanded by Italy, Serbia, Rumania, and Poland. However, the nationalities remaining in the former dual monarchy should have been assured an autonomy within a federation. And to such a federation there should have been attached the Catholic states of South Germany which were akin in culture and spirit to Austria—Bavaria, Baden, Württemberg, and Silesia.[12] This scheme bore a discernible resemblance to Marshal Foch's last stratagem of trying to detach the South German states from the Reich before the signing of the peace in June.

Perhaps the leading parliamentary exponent of Marshal Foch's Rhineland scheme was the rightist Deputy Maurice Barrès, President of the League of Patriots, who said: "We conceived of a different peace. . . . We expected the German frontier to be drawn at the Rhine, assuring us possession of the bridgeheads. This has been a fixed idea in the history of France." Barrès announced, to the surprise of many, that he would vote for the treaty, despite the disappointment which so many felt, "for the treaty contained the nucleus of greatness for European civilization and the guarantees of French security . . . provided these safeguards are not undermined, contradicted or weakened by those who have the duty of developing them—provided we have a Rhineland policy." Barrès advanced his threadbare argument that the Rhineland, so oriented toward France in its intellectual affinities, should be separated from Prussia and should enjoy an autonomy within Germany. "French intervention in the Rhineland," said Barrès, "should above all else be economic penetration. The government, labor unions, employer associations and chambers of commerce should work out an economic policy. There is an obvious community of economic interests between these regions and the rest of former Gaul." [13]

[12] *Annales,* 28 aout 1919, p. 3651.
[13] *Annales,* 28 aout 1919, p. 3644.

This unctuous language aroused the suspicion of Socialist Deputy Mistral, who was moved to reply:

I was somewhat surprised . . . to hear M. Barrès speak of *rapprochement* with Germany, or, more precisely, of a propaganda of *rapprochement* to be undertaken in the Rhenish provinces. . . . I fear that this policy of influence, of propaganda, of penetration of the Rhenish provinces, unless it is entirely disinterested and sincere, can arouse great distrust. I ask M. Barrès if we should believe in a complete change of heart on his part? Or, to the contrary, does he want to engage in a propaganda which, little by little, will tend to detach certain German elements in order, at a later date, to bring about total occupation, with another effort made to separate the Left bank of the Rhine and, if possible, to annex it to France? Such a policy would be full of the gravest dangers, and we explicitly denounce and condemn it.[14]

In the six weeks of debate, Clemenceau intervened on only one occasion, and that was on September 24–25, when a Havas agency dispatch carried the news from Washington that Senator Henry Cabot Lodge had obtained from the Senate, by 43 ballots to 40, a vote to postpone ratification until there could be a new study of the treaty.[15] This caused a sensation in the French Parliament, and compelled the Tiger to abandon his reticence. Until this provocation, the President of the Council had left the defense of the treaty to the skillful advocacy of peace delegate André Tardieu and Foreign Affairs Minister Stephen Pichon. Deputy Barthou, however, demanded of Clemenceau what assurances could be given Parliament and the nation that "if the American Senate did not ratify the treaty, there might nonetheless be guarantees which are indispensable for us? For my part, gentlemen, I fear that the treaty is a delusion. The question is in doubt. The Foreign Affairs Minister has not spoken to it, any more than M. Tardieu." [16]

Thus challenged, Clemenceau spoke for two sessions in defense of his diplomacy. He began with an explanation as to why he had allowed the debate to drag on for weeks. "Precisely because there

[14] *Annales,* 29 aout 1919, pp. 3659–3661.
[15] *Annales,* 4 septembre 1919, pp. 3735–3736.
[16] Beau de Loménie, *Le débat de ratification du traité de Versailles,* p. 175.

have been complaints that Parliament has not been properly informed, it would appear very bad grace to intervene to prevent
orators from speaking." He agreed with Barrès that "the drive
towards the Rhine was in the tradition of our ancestors." But no
one contemplated making the Germans of the Rhineland into
French citizens. Clemenceau argued that his memorandum of
February 25 had advocated a plan which would have left to the
Germans their own nationality while France would have had its
military frontier and its garrisons implanted on the Rhine. But the
Allies had strongly objected to this, and had offered a tripartite
treaty of guarantee in its stead. Moreover, there was no such thing
as an absolutely secure frontier. The Rhine itself had been crossed
a number of times. As for Germany, "it was a nation of 60 million
people. No one proposes breaking Germany's neck. We must live
with the Germans, even try to accommodate them. It is a question
which can hardly be solved except in the sense of accommoda-
tion." [17]

One of the most telling criticisms of Clemenceau's treaty came
from the avowed royalist, Jules Delahaye, who explained why his
group opposed the treaty. "We cannot vote for the treaty," he said,
"because the main defense of Monsieur Tardieu does not hold water.
In leaving Germany unified, you have wanted to remove from it
a motive for revenge. As if it were not revenge which it invoked
in the case of each of its aggressions. As if Germany had not styled
restitution each of its spoliations. As if the deliverance of Alsace-
Lorraine and Poland had not provided all the nationalistic pretexts
necessary. You have taken from them their ships, some of their
arms, their money, and their territory on the South, East and West.
You prohibit Anschluss with Austria. And you imagine that they
will not cry out in protest? Nothing could be more naive. Monsieur
Tardieu here has been guilty of criminal imprudence: the enemy
has been scotched, deeply irritated and humiliated, and yet you
leave him the instruments of power and vengeance." [18]

Prophetic words, but what did Delahaye actually want? Did he

[17] *Annales,* 24 septembre 1919, p. 4104.
[18] *Annales,* 25 septembre 1919, pp. 4126, 4132–4133.

favor the atomizing of Germany by France alone, when it had taken a coalition to defeat the enemy? It should be remembered that after the Second World War no less than four nations had to occupy Europe's second most numerous people. Could France, with only two-thirds of Germany's population, have done this alone—and against the strong opposition of its wartime Allies?

That Clemenceau had arranged the best peace possible in the straitened circumstances was the unenthusiastic viewpoint of most parliamentarians when the vote on the treaty was taken on October 2, 1919. The balloting recorded 372 votes for the treaty, 53 against, and 74 abstentions. Of those voting against the treaty, 51 were Socialists and two were rightists. Among the abstainers were a third of the Socialist deputies, the remainder being royalists and a few moderates.[19]

How does one account for the fact that so many of the deputies had voiced ringing approval of Marshal Foch's Rhineland scheme, and yet the great majority had voted for Clemenceau's compromise treaty? Because they would have preferred a detached Rhineland, given Anglo-American concurrence, but in default of that they shared Clemenceau's view that France should not be left alone to confront a still formidable Germany.

The polemic over the policy of German separatism, which had so embittered the relations between Foch and Poincaré on the one side and Clemenceau on the other, appeared to have subsided after parliamentary ratification of the treaty. But in 1922, several years after Clemenceau had given up the premiership and after he had been ignominiously defeated by a nonentity in the campaign for the presidency of the Republic, he announced plans for a trip to America. The aged patriot wanted to plead France's case before a quondam ally which had repudiated not only the promised tripartite treaty of military guarantee, but the Treaty of Versailles as well. When Marshal Foch heard of Clemenceau's proposed trip, he abandoned his soldierly reticence and gave a brutal interview to the New York *Tribune.* Foch predicted that once Clemenceau had arrived in America he would be lachrymose and sentimental, giving way to

[19] *Annales,* 1 octobre 1919, pp. 4270–4271.

the inevitable symptoms of advanced age. The marshal urged Clemenceau to stay at home, since he had manifestly lost the peace, and to forego soliciting sympathy from the Americans when none was forthcoming from the disabused French.

Clemenceau swallowed his wrath over this studied effrontery and waited seven years before retorting directly. What goaded him into a final counterattack upon Foch and Poincaré was the posthumous publication in 1929 of the marshal's apologia, *Le mémorial de Foch,* dictated just before Foch's death to Raymond Recouly. These recollections subsumed all of Foch's familiar grievances and complaints against Clemenceau, asserting that as peacemaker he had practically thrown away the victory which the marshal had so arduously won. Clemenceau, in a protracted spasm of fury which was to hasten his own departure within a year of the marshal's, wrote his rebuttal in *Grandeur and Misery of Victory.*

Clemenceau began his defense by comparing Foch with the Parthian archers of old, notorious for the cunning of their parting shots aimed over their shoulders. Foch's recollections, according to Clemenceau, were a veritable sheaf of poisoned arrows which the marshal had loosed against him just before Foch's disappearance into the sanctuary of the tomb. Clemenceau proceeded to excoriate Foch for having failed to utilize to the maximum his vast prestige as postwar chief technical adviser of a succession of war ministries. The marshal had within his power a peerless opportunity for calling to the attention of the world the repeated German mutilations of the treaty, yet Foch had remained mute on these patent dangers to French security. Nor had Foch helped provide France with what it could actually furnish itself—adequate frontier defenses. For ten years after the armistice of 1918, the "continuous line" school of strategic thought had been enshrined in French military circles. Then "fortified regions" supplanted this conception. This strategic plan (later to materialize as the Maginot Line) envisaged the massive fortification of France's northeastern frontier between Luxembourg and Switzerland by a defensive network of ferroconcrete and barbed wire barriers. Yet the marshal did not publicly protest the failure of successive French governments actually to build such static defenses, although the Maginot Line was debated in 1929 and projected on paper. (Clemenceau appeared as oblivious as Marshal Foch to the new offensive strategy of armored warfare by tanks and planes, to be elaborated definitively in 1934 by the obscure Colonel Charles de Gaulle, and to be adopted by the Germans.) Clemenceau charged that Foch, who in 1919 had made such a fetish of an "invincible frontier on the Rhine," appeared to lose all serious, sustained interest in France's eastern borders, once it was established that the marshal could not actually obtain the detachment of the Rhineland.[20]

And as for Foch's paladin, the fire-breathing Lorrainer, Poincaré, who was renowned as the advocate of three years of compulsory military service in 1913, he had become so complaisant a postwar politician, in Clemenceau's jaded view, that he declared before Parliament in April 1922 that at heart he wanted only one year of compulsory service. Poincaré continued to tack with the political wind when, in 1923, he sponsored a bill for a period of compulsory service as long as eighteen months. Such was the degree of militancy and vigilance displayed by the national guardian of 1919, who had made the welkin ring with cries of alarm about the "enduring German menace." France was being lulled into naive, complacent, disarmament at a time when the Reichswehr was already illicitly rearming Germany. What was Marshal Foch's reaction to the suicidal policy of national security pursued by his friend and champion, Poincaré? Discreet silence, if not outright concurrence in its heedlessness and fatuousness.

Clemenceau intimated that Poincaré, after 1924, appeared to lose all interest in his former fixation, the question of Rhineland separatism. There had been a general recrudescence of separatism in West Germany in 1923, when Premier Poincaré ordered the Ruhr occupied by French troops even as the Americans withdrew their occupation forces from the Rhineland. These two events revived the hopes of the sanguine, tireless Dr. Dorten in Wiesbaden. Meanwhile even more obscure separatist competitors emerged in Düsseldorf under the leadership of Joseph Matthes, and in Cologne under a hotheaded war invalid, Joseph Smeets, who attracted a minor

[20] Clemenceau, *Grandeur and Misery*, pp. 356–362.

following. Dorten induced his rivals to merge with his separatists in a United Rhenish Party at Mainz. But the harmony was brief, for on September 30, 1923 nearly a hundred separatists were massacred at Düsseldorf by Prussian police, with the British refusing to intervene in an "internal" German affair.

A month later, a Rhenish republic was again proclaimed, this time at Aachen in the Belgian zone. But schism immediately developed between the new separatist leader of this zone, Leo Deckers, and Dr. Dorten and Joseph Matthes. This time the British were not so reluctant to intervene, for they quickly suppressed the Deckers' Aachen regime, while German Free Corps terrorists killed several hundred separatists in the vicinity of Bonn on November 15, 1923.

The *rigor mortis* of separatism set in on February 12, 1924, at Pirmasens in the Palatinate. In this industrial town, where there was stationed a small French force of twenty-five Moroccans under a sergeant-major, a mob of three hundred German nationalists, abetted by the local police and firemen, besieged forty separatists in the subprefecture building, which was set on fire. As the separatists tried to surrender, they were butchered and their bodies burned before a company of French riflemen could reach Pirmasens to restore order. Clemenceau concluded his account of the *ignis fatuus* of separatism with the contemptuous notation: "And M. Poincaré, who was Prime Minister when these events took place at Pirmasens, never again spoke of this 'movement' for an independent Rhineland: there are memories it is better to leave asleep." [21]

For all of the jeremiads of Foch and Poincaré against the compromise peace treaty, Clemenceau had salvaged for France as much as was possible in the dismal circumstances. As Professor Denis W. Brogan has expressed it:

The veteran Clemenceau was almost alone in his pessimistic wisdom. He knew that without British and American support, it was impossible effectively to restrain German power. Therefore he gave up the tangible guarantees of victory and security wanted by the soldiers, the separation of the Rhineland from Germany, the permanent occupation of key fortresses, for an Anglo-American guarantee of the new borders. He could

[21] Clemenceau, p. 231.

not believe that the American people would repudiate their President. They did, and the foolish rulers of Britain cheerfully took the chance to get out of their share in the guarantee. The average Frenchman thought he had been cheated; he had.[22]

Despite these undeniable truths, France still had the great advantage of the right of unilateral reoccupation of the Rhineland in case Germany violated the Treaty of Versailles. That the pusillanimous Sarraut-Flandin Cabinet chose not to use this invaluable weapon in March 1936, when Hitler reoccupied the Rhineland, was not the responsibility of Clemenceau. Furthermore, Clemenceau's renunciation of a detached Rhineland and his "trusting" acceptance of the proffered tripartite treaty of military guarantee had made the moral basis of the Anglo-American repudiation of that promise completely untenable. Later, when Nazi Germany threatened France and the whole fabric of western civilization, the festering Anglo-American conscience, reinforced by the belated realization of the Nazi menace to their own existence, galvanized the English-speaking world into a renewed solidarity with France—a *rapprochement* which would have been precluded by a disguised or overt French annexation of the Rhineland.

The outcome of Clemenceau's Rhineland policy by 1940 was admittedly a defeat. By then France's security policy was a shambles. No more than Foch had Clemenceau been a vociferous advocate of a modern strategy of the lightning offensive carried out by armored divisions and by strategic air bombardment. Yet the aged statesman seemed to have descried at least the outlines of new weapons systems when he asked his Cabinet, on April 25, 1919, "Would our presence on the Rhine prevent German planes from coming to destroy our cities, if Germany could rebuild an air force?" But he never developed any new, integrated strategy involving the use of tanks and planes, as Colonel de Gaulle was to do in the 1930's. The failure to appreciate fully the possibilities of the tank and plane was all the more culpable on the part of professional soldier Foch—especially since he had made such a fetish of the attack during 1914–1918.

[22] Denis W. Brogan, *The French Nation From Napoleon to Pétain* (New York, 1957), pp. 247–248.

France's postwar treaty commitments to Belgium, Poland, Czechoslovakia, Rumania, and Yugoslavia had clearly called for an offensive strategy. But obsessed, doubtlessly, with the memory of the hecatombs of 1914–1918, both Clemenceau and Foch adhered to a military policy of static defense and the war of "limited liability." Foch wanted the defense line drawn along the Rhine, well within Germany, where it would have had to be manned by France in isolation. Clemenceau likewise relied on a static defense line, but one staked out along a frontier indisputably French, which would not have precluded the concurrence, or even the active support, of allies. Both great men erred gravely as to he adequacy of a static defense. But the differing Rhineland policies of Clemenceau and Foch nevertheless gave France two choices. With Clemenceau's conception France, in event of need, could put to courageous use a morally and legally valid policy with at least the acquiescence, and perhaps the participation, of allies. With Foch's policy France would have to engage in a suicidal struggle in complete moral, military, and diplomatic isolation. Such being the formidable alternatives, fortunately Clemenceau prevailed.

Bibliographical Note

Index

Bibliographical Note

In carrying forward the study of French civil-military relations from the war years into the Peace Conference, one is immediately struck with the drying up of many of the wartime source materials. One notes with regret that even the *Journal officiel de la République Française* was silent on the vital Rhineland question, apart from a few fugitive references, until the ratification debates began on August 26, 1919. Most of the writers of wartime diaries, reminiscences, and autobiographies laid down their pens on November 11, 1918. Raymond Poincaré, for example, did not extend beyond 1918 *Au service de la France: neuf années de souvenirs* (10 vols., Paris 1926–33). Nor did the liaison officer Colonel Emile E. Herbillon continue beyond the armistice his invaluable *Souvenirs d'un officier de liaison pendant la guerre mondiale* (Paris, 1930).

Fortunately for the purpose of the present study, the protagonists of the politico-military drama continued their apologias through the Versailles Conference. Marshal Ferdinand Foch, although terminating with the armistice his *Mémoires pour servir a l'histoire de la guerre de 1914–1918* (2 vols., Paris, 1931), carried his polemic with Clemenceau through June 1919 in a work in large part dictated to Raymond Recouly, *Le mémorial de Foch: mes entretiens avec le maréchal* (Paris, 1929). Georges Clemenceau replied, measure for measure, in *Grandeur et misères d'une victoire* (Paris, 1930) [English translation, *Grandeur and Misery of Victory* (New York, 1930)].

Of inestimable worth to this monograph in furnishing evidence of French incitement of Rhenish separatism were the recently opened Henry T. Allen Papers, 1919, Library of Congress, Washington, D.C. Also of use on this issue were the Woodrow Wilson Papers, 1919; the Henry White Papers, 1919; the Tasker H. Bliss Papers, 1919; the John J. Pershing Papers, 1919; and the Ray Stannard Baker Papers, 1919—all of the Library of Congress, Washington, D.C. Much light was thrown upon the Rhineland dispute by David Lloyd George in *The Truth About the Peace Treaties* (London, 1938). The three-volume work of Ray Stannard Baker, *Woodrow Wilson and World Settlement* (Garden City, N.Y., 1922), was of value in revealing the American position on the Rhineland scheme of Foch. Clemenceau's military adviser and friend, General Jean Jules Mordacq, produced a four-volume work germane to this monograph topic, *Le ministère Clemenceau: journal d'un témoin* (Paris, 1931). The private secretary of Clemenceau, Jean Martet, likewise disclosed relevant primary evidence in *La mort du Tigre* (Paris, 1930) [English translation, *Georges Clemenceau* (London, 1930)]. Edward M. House and Charles Seymour adduced some testimony in Charles Seymour, ed., *The Intimate Papers of Colonel House* (4 vols., New York, 1928), and in Edward M. House and Charles Seymour, eds., *What Really Happened at Paris* (New York, 1921). Of fundamental importance was the recently published two-volume collection of stenographic notes of the secretary of the Big Four sessions at the Peace Conference, Paul Mantoux, ed., *Les délibérations du conseil des quatre* (Paris, 1955). Of comparable usefulness was the apologia of Clemenceau's supporter, Peace Conference delegate André Tardieu, *La paix* (Paris, 1921) [English translation, *The Truth About the Treaty* (Indianapolis, 1921)]. Primary source material was likewise found 'in the work of Gabriel Terrail [Mermeix, pseud.], *Le combat des trois: notes et documents sur la conférence de la paix* (Paris, 1922).

French and German primary material on the Rhenish and Palatine separatist movements was none too abundant. Basic was the testimony of the protagonist, Hans A. Dorten, *La tragédie rhénane* (Paris, 1945). Surprisingly, of less value were the Hans Adam Dorten Papers in The Hoover Institution on War, Revolution, and Peace at Palo Alto, California. This collection is largely made up of attestations from several-score Rhenish mayors, curates, directors of peasant unions, and leaders of the Nassau Center Party, in favor of a plebiscite on the creation of a Rhenish Republic within the German Reich. The similarity of phraseology of the attestations suggests propagandistic "coaching," perhaps by the Hesse-Nassau Committee and the Mid-Rhine Committee, both organized by Dorten. Of greater importance was the article by Dorten, "Le général Mangin en Rhénanie," *Revue des deux mondes* (July 1, 1937). Of inestimable value were the admissions of General Charles Mangin in "Lettres de Rhénanie," *La Revue de Paris* (April 1, 1936). A staff officer of General Gérard, Major Paul Jacquot, unintentionally threw light upon the dubious role of the French occupying authorities in the Palatinate in *General Gérard und die Pfalz* (Berlin, 1920).

I was able to elicit a brief statement on separatism from Konrad Adenauer in a letter from him, dated 5 September 1956. An account of Dorten's coup was published in the work of the so-called Provisional Government of the Rhineland Republic in Wiesbaden, *Die Rheinische Republik: Die Gruende fuer die Errichtung eines Rheinischen Friestaates und die Vorgeschichte der Proklamation vom 1, Juni 1919* (Wiesbaden, 1919). A member of the German Democratic Party who quickly turned against separatism, Fritz Brüggemann, gave a detailed description of the role of the Catholic Centrists in agitating for a Rhenish Republic in *Die Rheinische Republik* (Bonn, 1919). The Bavarian State Commissioner for the Palatinate threw light upon the Palatine separatist efforts of General Gérard and Dr. Eberhard Haas in *Die Pfalz unter französischer Besetzung 1918–1924* (München, 1925). Administrative President von Winterstein published a brief version of the Haas putsch, "Der 18 Mai 1919, ein Gedenktag der pfälzischen Geschichte," in *Dokumente aus dem Befreiungskampf der Pfalz*, Pfälzische Rundschau, 1930. In the same issue of Pfälzische Rundschau there also appeared a short article by von Winterstein's successor as Administrative President, Friedrich von Chlingensperg, "Ein Musterbeispiel französischer Gewaltpolitik."

Primary material on the background of this monograph topic included a number of wartime French books which proposed, in one form or another, the detachment of the Rhineland: Onésime Reclus, *Le Rhin français. Annexion de la rive gauche. Sa moralité. Sa necessité. Ses avantages.* (Paris, 1915); Onésime Reclus, *L'Allemagne en morceau: paix draconienne* (Paris, 1915); Abbé Stephen Coubé, *Alsace, Lorraine et France rhénane: exposé des droits historiques de la France sur toute la rive gauche du Rhin* (Paris, 1915); Louis Dimier, *Les troncons du serpent: idée d'une dislocation de l'empire allemand et d'une reconstitution des Allemagnes* (Paris, 1915); C. M. Savarit, *La frontière du Rhin* (Paris, 1915); Ernest Babelon, *Le Rhin dans l'histoire* (2 vols., Paris, 1916–1917); F. de Grailly, *La verité territoriale et la rive gauche du Rhin* (Paris, 1917); Georges Blondel, *La Rhénanie: son passé: son avenir* (Paris, 1921); Major Espérandieu, *Le Rhin français* (Paris, 1915); Albert de Pouvourville, *Jusq'au Rhin: les terres meurtries et les terres promises* (Paris, 1919); J. Dontenville, *Après la guerre: les Allemagnes, la France, la Belgique et la Hollande* (Paris, 1915); Alphonse Aulard, *La paix future d'après la révolution française et Kant* (Paris, 1916); Edouard Driault, *Les traditions politiques de la France et les conditions de la paix* (Paris, 1916); Edouard Driault, *La République et le Rhin* (Paris, 1916); Charles Stiénon, *La rive gauche du Rhin et l'equilibre européen* (Paris, 1917); Vidal de la Blache, *La France de l'Est* (Paris, 1917); and Philippe Sagnac, *Le Rhin français pendant la révolution et l'empire* (Paris, 1917).

Newspapers used in this study were the *Kölnische Zeitung*, 1919; *Kölnische Volkszeitung*, 1919; *Frankfurter Zeitung*, 1919; *Rheinisch-Westfälische Zeitung*, 1919; *Le Matin*, 1919; *Le Temps*, 1919; *L'Echo de Paris*, 1919; *The Daily Mail*, 1919.

Primary works of incidental relevance to Foch's Rhineland scheme were George E. R. Gedye, *The Revolver Republic* (London, 1930), written by a British journalist who had been an intelligence officer at Cologne in 1919; Charles Bugnet, *Foch Speaks* (New York, 1929), containing several relevant anecdotes and quotations; Joseph Paul-Boncour, *Entre deux guerres: souvenirs sur la IIIe république* (2 vols., Paris, 1945), which stated the Socialist position on a detached Rhineland; Jules Cambon, "La paix: notes inédites, 1919," *La Revue de Paris* (November 1, 1937), containing a retrospective appraisal by a Peace Conference delegate of the Foch-Clemenceau dispute; Charles E. Callwell, *Field Marshal Sir Henry Wilson* (2 vols., New York, 1927), which quoted Foch's complaints about not being informed by Clemenceau; Henry

T. Allen, *The Rhineland Occupation* (Indianapolis, 1927), in which the American occupation commander described Dorten's efforts to win American and British support for his *coup d'état;* General Nudant, "A Spa: journal du président de la commission interallié d'armistice (1918–1919)," *La Revue de France* (April 1, 1925), which set forth German complaints against Dorten's *putsch;* Hunter Liggett, *Commanding an American Army* (Boston, 1925), which described Dorten's efforts to win American support; and Pierrepont B. Noyes, *While Europe Waits for Peace* (New York, 1921), the testimony of an American political officer in the Rhineland which revealed the degree of American confusion over the separatists' identity and aims.

The French secondary works bearing on Foch's Rhineland scheme included the following: Maurice Barrès, *Les grandes problèmes du Rhin* (Paris, 1930); Georges Vial-Mazel, *Erreurs et oublis de Georges Clemenceau: L'affaire du Rhin* (Paris, 1931); Guy de Traversay, "La première tentative de République rhénane," *La Revue de Paris* (November 15 and December 1, 1928); Raymond Recouly, *La barrière du Rhin* (Paris, 1923); Joseph Aulneau, *Le Rhin et la France* (Paris, 1921); Paul Binoux, *La question rhénane et la France* (Paris, 1921); Georges Vial-Mazel, *Le Rhin: victoire allemande* (Paris, 1921); Major Louis Eugène Mangin, *La France et le Rhin* (Genève, 1945); Major René Michel Lhopital, *Foch, l'armistice et la paix* (Paris, 1938); and E. Beau de Lomenie, *Le débat de ratification du traité de Versailles* (Paris, 1945).

German secondary accounts included Leo Böhmer, *Die Rheinische Separatistenbewegung und die französische Presse* (Stuttgart, 1928); Erich H. Kaden and Max Springer, *Der politischen Charakter der französischen Kulturpropaganda am Rhein* (Berlin, 1920); Friedrich Grimm, *Poincaré am Rhein* (Berlin, 1940); Paul Weymar, *Konrad Adenauer* (München, 1955); Robert Oberhauser, *Kampf der Westmarck* (Neustadt an der Haardt, 1934); Erwin Goebel, *Die pfälzische Presse im Abwehrkampf der Pfalz gegen Franzosen und Separatisten 1918–1924* (Ludwigshafen, 1931); Paul Grossmann, *Im Kampf um den Rhein 1918–1930* (Frankfort am Main, 1933); and Bruno Kuske, *Rheingrenze und Pufferstaat* (Bonn, 1919).

There should be mentioned two biographies by English writers: Basil H. Liddell Hart, *Foch: The Man of Orleans* (Boston, 1932), perhaps the best sketch of the marshal; George Aston, *Marshal Foch* (New York, 1929), a much slighter work. Two American monographs were of some value: George B. Noble, *Policies and Opinions at Paris* (New York, 1935); Ebba Dahlin, *French and German Public Opinion on Declared War Aims* (Stanford University, Calif., 1933).

Index

Harvard Historical Monographs

21. The Election to the Russian Constituent Assembly of 1917. By O. H. Radkey. 1950.
22. Conversion and the Poll Tax in Early Islam. By Daniel C. Dennett. 1950.*
23. Albert Gallatin and the Oregon Problem. By Frederick Merk. 1950.
24. The Incidence of the Emigration during the French Revolution. By Donald Greer. 1951.*
25. Alterations of the Words of Jesus as Quoted in the Literature of the Second Century. By Leon E. Wright. 1952.*
26. Liang Ch'i Ch'ao and the Mind of Modern China. By Joseph R. Levenson. 1953.*
27. The Japanese and Sun Yat-sen. By Marius B. Jansen. 1954.
28. English Politics in the Early Eighteenth Century. By Robert Walcott, Jr. 1956.*
29. The Founding of the French Socialist Party (1893-1905). By Aaron Noland. 1956.
30. British Labour and the Russian Revolution, 1917–1924. By Stephen Richards Graubard. 1956.
31. RKFDV: German Resettlement and Population Policy. By Robert L. Koehl. 1957.
32. Disarmament and Peace in British Politics, 1914–1919. By Gerda Richards Crosby. 1957.
33. Concordia Mundi: The Career and Thought of Guillaume Postel (1510–1581). By W. J. Bouwsma. 1957.
34. Bureaucracy, Aristocracy, and Autocracy. The Prussian Experience, 1660–1815. By Hans Rosenberg. 1958.
35. Exeter, 1540–1640. The Growth of an English County Town. By Wallace T. MacCaffrey. 1958.
36. Historical Pessimism in the French Enlightenment. By Henry Vyverberg. 1958.
37. The Renaissance Idea of Wisdom. By Eugene F. Rice, Jr. 1958.
38. The First Professional Revolutionist: Filippo Michele Buonarroti (1761–1837). By Elizabeth L. Eisenstein. 1959.
39. The Formation of the Baltic States: A Study of the Effects of Great Power Politics upon the Emergence of Lithuania, Latvia, and Estonia. By Stanley W. Page. 1959.
40. Conservation and the Gospel of Efficiency: The Progressive Conservation Movement, 1890–1920. By Samuel P. Hays. 1959.
41. The Urban Frontier: The Rise of Western Cities, 1790–1830. By Richard C. Wade. 1959.
42. New Zealand, 1769–1840: Early Years of Western Contact. By Harrison M. Wright. 1959.
43. Ottoman Imperialism and German Protestantism, 1521–1555. By Stephen A. Fischer-Galati. 1959.
44. Foch versus Clemenceau: France and German Dismemberment, 1918–1919. By Jere Clemens King. 1960.